ISBN 978-1-333-51170-8
PIBN 10513694

1 MONTH OF
FREE
READING

at

www.ForgottenBooks.com

By purchasing this book you are eligible for one month membership to ForgottenBooks.com, giving you unlimited access to our entire collection of over 700,000 titles via our web site and mobile apps.

To claim your free month visit:

www.forgottenbooks.com/free513694

English
Français
Deutsche
Italiano
Español
Português

www.forgottenbooks.com

Mythology Photography **Fiction**
Fishing Christianity **Art** Cooking
Essays Buddhism Freemasonry
Medicine **Biology** Music **Ancient
Egypt** Evolution Carpentry Physics
Dance Geology **Mathematics** Fitness
Shakespeare **Folklore** Yoga Marketing
Confidence Immortality Biographies
Poetry **Psychology** Witchcraft
Electronics Chemistry History **Law**
Accounting **Philosophy** Anthropology
Alchemy Drama Quantum Mechanics
Atheism Sexual Health **Ancient History**
Entrepreneurship Languages Sport
Paleontology Needlework Islam
Metaphysics Investment Archaeology
Parenting Statistics Criminology
Motivational

AT TWENTY-FIVE.

FANNY CROSBY'S

LIFE - STORY

BY HERSELF

NEW YORK:

EVERY WHERE PUBLISHING COMPANY

1903

DEDICATED

TO ALL MY FRIENDS

IN BOTH WORLDS

INTRODUCTION: BY WILL CARLETON.

All over this country, and, one might say, the world, Fanny Crosby's hymns are singing themselves into the hearts and souls of the people. They have been doing this for many years, and will do so as long as our civilization lasts. There are to-day used in religious meetings, more of her inspired lines, than of any other poet, living or dead. Not only those hymns with which she is credited in the singing-books, but thousands of others, have come from her heart and mind; for she has written, not only under her own name, but several nom-de-plumes. Her sacred lyrics have been translated into several languages. She is easily the greatest living writer of hymns, and will always occupy a high place among authors.

But what of Fanny Crosby the woman? Is her personality as sweet and inspiring as her poems? Has her life been an exemplification and illustration of them?

From those of us that know her well, such questions would elicit a smile. Whoever has had opportunity of witnessing her patience, her sweetness of thought and life, her bright winsomeness and her all-around and all-through goodness, would not even take the trouble to answer in the affirmative; he would say, "There she is; there is her life; let them speak for themselves."

But compared to the thousands that have sung her inspiring hymns and partaken of her gentle spirit, few, of course, can have the opportunity of knowing her personally; and it is natural that all should wish to learn as much about her as possible.

Introduction.

In this book is an account of her life, told by herself, and as she only could tell it. There are several of her newest hymns; a few of the many tributes that she has received; and the latest portrait of her, taken expressly for this book. Every copy of the work that is sold, adds substantially and immediately to the comfort of this grand woman, who has been singing in such far-reaching tones, the praise of her God and her Christ, for sixty years.

The response will, no doubt, be such as to convince our dear Fanny Crosby that she occupies a warm place in the hearts of the people, and that she is sure of their love, their honor, and their practical appreciation.

CONTENTS.

vii

Contents.

viii

Contents.

Contents.

Contents.

Contents.

CHAPTER I.—1820-1825.

INFANCY—BLINDED AT SIX WEEKS OF AGE—AM
THANKFUL FOR IT NOW—PARENTS AND RELA-
TIVES—LONELY AMUSEMENTS—ASKING GOD
FOR A CHANCE IN THE WORLD—HIS ANSWER
—THE BELLIGERENT LAMB—DANIEL DREW'S
ATTEMPTED PRESENT OF "STOCK."

IT seemed intended by the blesséd Provi-
dence of God, that I should be blind all
my life; and I thank Him for the dispen-
sation. I was born with a pair of as good
eyes as any baby ever owned; but when I was
six weeks of age, a slight touch of inflamma-
tion came upon them: and they were put under
the care of a physician.

What he did to them, or what happened in
spite of him, I do not know, but it resulted in
their permanent destruction, so far as seeing is
concerned; and I was doomed to blindness all
the rest of my earthly existence.

I have heard that this physician never ceased
expressing his regret at the occurrence; and
that it was one of the sorrows of his life. But
if I could meet him now, I would say, "Thank
you, thank you—over and over again—for
making me blind, if it was through your
agency that it came about!"

This sounds strangely to you, reader? But I assure you I mean it—every word of it; and if perfect earthly sight were offered me to-morrow, I would not accept it. Did you ever know of a blind person's talking like this before?

Why would I not have that doctor's mistake —if mistake it was—remedied? Well, there are many reasons: and I will tell you some of them.

One is, that I know, although it may have been a blunder on the physician's part, it was no mistake of God's. I verily believe it was His intention that I should live my days in physical darkness, so as to be better prepared to sing His praises and incite others so to do. I could not have written thousands of hymns—many of which, if you will pardon me for repeating it, are sung all over the world— if I had been hindered by the distractions of seeing all the interesting and beautiful objects that would have been presented to my notice.

Another reason is, that, while I am deprived of many splendid sights (which, as above mentioned, might draw me away from the principal work of my life), I have also been spared the seeing of a great many unpleasant things. The merciful God has put His hand over my eyes, and shut out from me the sight of many instances of cruelty and bitter unkindness and misfortune, that I would not have been able to relieve, and must simply have suffered in seeing. I am content with what I can know of life through the four senses I possess, practically unimpaired, at eighty-three years of age. Hearing, tasting, smelling, and feeling, are still felt, in their fullest degree.

Another reason for my apparently strange assertion is, that I have been able to test and make sure so many kind and loving friends. Almost without exception, the great world has been good to me : all the kinder, perhaps, on account of what it considered my affliction. I may say truly that I never for a moment presumed on my blindness for any extra courtesy or advantage, yet I have often felt that it was a bond between sympathetic hearts and mine.

I was born in Putnam County, N. Y., March 24, 1820. My father's name was John Crosby : he died when I was very young. My grandfather fought in the War of 1812; my great-grandfather in the Revolution. My mother's given name was the good old-fashioned one of Mercy.

I have always been proud at having been related, though not very nearly, to that famous hero of the Revolution, Enoch Crosby. I have often sat when a little child, and listened to stories of his courage and heroism. Though he never came to be an officer, yet it was universally admitted that he did the Revolutionary cause more good than many a gallant general. One of Cooper's most famous novels has him for its hero. He lies buried now, in a little country cemetery near Carmel, N. Y., with scores of my race sleeping around him.

As a child, although blind, I was by no means helpless, or of a sedentary disposition : I indulged in many of the sports enjoyed by my little playmates, and romped and clambered wherever they did. I could climb a tree or ride a horse as well as any of them, and many good people when seeing me at play were surprised at being told of my "misfortune." I attended school at times, but, of course, could not study: raised letters for the blind were not common then.

One of my principal amusements was to sit with hands clasped, or engaged in some piece of work with needles, and listen to the many voices of Nature. The laughing and sighing of the wind—the sobbing of the storm—the rippling of water—the "rain on the roof"—the artillery of the thunder—all impressed me more than I can tell. I lived many lives with my imagination. Sometimes I was a sailor, standing at the mast-head, and looking out into the storm; sometimes a general, leading armies to battle; then a clergyman, addressing large audiences and pleading with them to come to Christ; then the leader of a gigantic choir of voices, singing praises to God. My ambition was boundless; my desires were intense to live for some great purpose in the world, and to make for myself a name that should endure; but in what manner was it to be done?

A poor little blind girl, without influential friends, could have as many ambitions as any one; but how was she to achieve them? What was there for her? The great world that could see, was rushing past me day by day, and sweeping on toward the goal of its necessities and desires; while I was left stranded by the

wayside. "Oh, you cannot do this—because
you are blind, you know; you can never go
there, because it would not be worth while:
you could not see anything if you did, you
know":—these and other things were often
said to me, in reply to my many and eager
questionings.

Often, when such circumstances as this made
me very blue and depressed, I would creep off
alone, kneel down, and ask God if, though
blind, I was not one of His children; if in all
His great world He had not some little place
for me; and it often seemed that I could hear
Him say, "Do not be discouraged, little girl:
you shall some day be happy and useful, even in
your blindness." And I would go back among
my associates, cheered and encouraged; and
feeling that it would not be very long before
my life would be full of activity and usefulness.

And so it was, that gradually I began to lose
my regret and sorrow at having been robbed
of sight: little by little God's promises and
consolations came throbbing into my mind.
Not only the Scriptures, but the hymns that I
heard sung Sabbath after Sabbath, made deep
impressions upon me.

With the ultra-acute hearing which generally accompanies blindness, I could distinguish
every word of the hymns, however indistinctly
they might be sung; and they were in many
cases a refreshment to my young soul. Even
in childhood, I began to wonder who made
those hymns; and if I myself could ever make
one that people would sing.

17

As already indicated, a growing, healthy girl, although she may be blind, cannot live entirely in her intellectual nature: and I did not lack means for my share of the regulation juvenile sports. I dare say I was as bothersome to my mother as are most children to theirs; and was constantly asking for some novel way by which to amuse myself.

One day she called me to her side, and said, "Here, Fanny, is a *live* toy: only be careful of it and not hurt it."

It was a sweet, lovely pet lamb !—and I seriously thought, for a day or two, of having my name changed to "Mary", of whom I had heard as once possessing a similar piece of property, and of smuggling the dear little pet away to some school, to see if the teacher would turn it out, and if it would then linger near, etc. I finally gave up the idea, but I played with my little quadrupedal toy morning, noon, and night: until at last the sturdy creature got into the habit of playfully butting me over, as one of its pastimes.

Now came the first tragedy of my life: after maltreating me several times, and being promptly forgiven on each occasion by its loving victim, the "lamb", which was now fast assuming the proportions of sheephood, became the subject of a star-chamber trial, and was condemned to death, and to punishment after death: to be cooked and eaten. Be sure most of it was done before I knew anything about it: else probably I should have raised the roof. The first I knew about it, I was told we were to have lamb-chop for dinner: and in the ominous silence that followed, I divined my favorite's fate. Tears and fasting followed, but they were of no avail: the belligerent little friend was no more.

Daniel Drew, afterwards a celebrated railroad magnate, but then a drover, dealing in an entirely different kind of stock, often passed our house with droves of sheep and cattle. We were always great friends: and soon after the above-mentioned sad event, he came into our house and placed a small lamb in my arms, saying, "Here, Fanny, is a present for you"; but I had no heart then to accept it, and declined the gift, to his great surprise.

CHAPTER II.—1825.

A SLOOP-JOURNEY DOWN THE HUDSON—ACTING
AS CAPTAIN'S FIRST MATE—A PATRIOTIC
SONG—DRS. MOTT AND DELAFIELD GIVE AD-
VERSE DECISION—BLIND FOR LIFE!—THE
SAD JOURNEY HOME—WHAT THE WAVES SAID.

ONE evening, when I was about five years old, my good mother called me to her from the dooryard, where I had been playing, and I ran to her side. As I say, it was evening, but that made no difference with me: I could play in the night as well as daytime, and had no trouble in reaching her side, whether the candles were lighted or not. There were no kerosene lamps then, and people in the country had to depend for their light upon candles, made by dipping a wick of cotton repeatedly in melted tallow, until enough of it clung to the wick to make a "body" for the apparatus; and when that was lighted it did not illuminate a house to any great extent.

Well, my dear mother called me to her side, and said: "Fanny, I am going to take you on a little journey. We shall travel first in a wagon, till we come to the bank of a beautiful river, with mountains on each side of it; then

20

we shall get into a sail-boat and sail south for many miles; then we shall come to a great city, larger than anything of which you have ever heard or thought, and stay there for several days; and then home again."

The idea of taking a journey filled me with joy, and I danced about the room with perhaps not enough attention to the furniture that kept getting in the way; but my transports were somewhat modified, when she explained the object of the expedition—to have a surgical operation performed upon my eyes. "There may be some pain with it, Fanny," she explained: "but you are willing to bear it, are you not?"

I already knew what pain was :—it is, alas! one of the first things we learn in life! and I shrank a little at the idea of any of it being inflicted upon me. "But, Fanny," my mother explained, "perhaps it will result in giving you your sight: so that you can see everything that is around you, and play with the rest of the children exactly as they do, study pretty pictures, and read interesting books, and enjoy yourself in a hundred ways that you do not, as your eyes are now." Then I was happy again.

This was in 1825; and you may readily believe that means of communication were not many and varied, in those days. There was not even a stage from our home or from near there, to any point upon the Hudson River.

We started one morning before the early dawn was in the skies, and rode in a market-wagon to Sing Sing, on the Hudson, where we were to take a sloop for New York; steamboats were still very few and far between. This musically-named town, in which I thought every one, probably, belonged to the choir, was then a small country hamlet, straggling along the banks of the river—with no idea that it would ever bear such a prominent part in the punishment of the malefactors of a great commonwealth.

So at four o'clock in the soft dawn of that summer morning, we unfurled our sails, and went rushing down the river toward the great metropolis. It is perhaps needless to say that the novel experience was a delight to me: I was all over the deck, and soon, I may safely say, in the good graces of everybody aboard. I could not of course view the beautiful scenery through which we were passing; but there were plenty of friends to describe it to me, and I enjoyed it upon the whole as much perhaps as if I could have seen, and as if I had had to depend entirely upon my own powers of observation. I have always delighted in passing through beautiful scenery, and, indeed, enjoyed the sensation of traveling—perhaps more than some that can see; and I find that other blind people are the same in this respect.

My poor mother was at times seasick, or, more accurately expressing it, river-sick: but I kept well, and after knowing that she was comfortable in her berth, and being told that nobody ever died of that kind of sickness, and that she would be all the better for it soon, I was the gayest of the gay; and Captain Green immediately adopted me as "first mate of the sloop." I was, I believe, called a fairly pretty child; and my black curls and frisky manners did not detract from the five-year-old disposition that developed in me, to be the belle of the company.

The dear old Captain pretended to discover that I was a great vocalist; and at times kept me busy singing all the little songs I had gathered up since old enough to learn and understand them. These were not very many or particularly deep; but they served. One of them I remember inaugurated itself with the following impressive lines, sung to a famous patriotic air:

> "I wish I was a Yankee's wife,
>   And then I would have *somethin'* ·
> Every fall an ear of corn,
>   And now and then a *pumkin!*"

I felt, even then, that there was something a little irregular in the rhyming of this stanza: but the Captain pretended to hold my song particularly in very high esteem, and whenever he was a little blue, called me to him and coaxed or hired me to sing it. With the usual thrift of the accomplished cantatrice, I gradually increased my prices as the article grew more and more in dem; nd; and was very much disappointed when, a′ er gliding through the beautiful Highlands and past the impressive palisades, we arrived in the Big City.

It was early in the morning when we landed,

having been twenty-four hours in making the trip from Sing Sing—a journey that I have frequently performed since, by railroad, in fifty-five minutes.

We went to the house of a friend who bore the good old name of Jacob Smith, at No. 10 Roosevelt Street, a very fine place at that time; and soon we were in the presence of the famous Dr. Valentine Mott. 1 felt that Dr. Mott had a kind, pleasant face: singularly enough I have always been able to form a pretty accurate opinion of a countenance, by the voice that proceeded from it.

Being but a little child, to whom one of God's creatures was about the same as another, except as they pleased or displeased me, I did not stand so much in awe of the great Dr. Mott; but my mother did, and listened with bated breath to hear what he should say of my case. It was not the first time that poor mortals had hung upon his words; for he was even then considered the foremost surgeon of his time. He occupied the chair of surgery in Columbia College, and had performed operations that no other practitioner ever dared to undertake. He had, seven years before, placed a ligature around the brachiocephalic trunk, or arteria innominata, only two inches from the heart, for aneurism of the right sub-clavian artery; and that for the first time in the history of surgery. To be sure the patient died within a month; but with the comforting assurance that he had had something done to him with a knife, that no other patient had ever experienced. And as this was before the age of chloroform, or any other very effective anæsthetics, death must certainly have been a relief.

Well, Dr. Mott and another celebrated surgeon at that time, named Dr. Delafield, examined my eyes and told my tearfully-listening mother, that there was no hope for them: malpractice had spoiled them. And so we returned to our country home—taking the same sloop and the same market-wagon as those in which we had come.

The poor doctor who had spoiled my eyes, soon disappeared from the neighborhood; and we never heard any more about him. He is probably dead, before this time; but if I could ever meet him, I would tell him that he unwittingly did me the greatest favor in the world.

I was more thoughtful and sad on the way back up the river: the great doctor had not been above placing his fatherly hand on my head, and saying, "Poor little girl!" and that touch of sympathy went with me as I journeyed homeward. Hour after hour, when I had crept into my little "bunk" on the sloop, I heard the dear waves of the river singing to me, and telling me not to be discouraged. "Fanny, be brave! Fanny, be brave!" they seemed to say: "brighter days will come yet!"

And, indeed, they were coming: although from what direction I did not then know. But I never lost my faith in the great Father above; I knew that the river-waves were His, and that I had heard His voice.

BIBLE-INSTRUCTION — MY FIRST POEM —— MY
FIRST LITERARY ADMIRER—HIS INABILITY TO
CONCEAL HIS SENTIMENTS — A TERRIBLE
THIRST FOR KNOWLEDGE—A PLEA FOR MEN-
TAL LIGHT—GOD'S GOODNESS IN ANSWERING
PRAYER.

THE greatest piece of good fortune that
attended me when a little girl. was
that I was taught the Bible—line upon
line, and precept upon precept. When
nine years old we moved to Ridgefield, Connecticut, and there lived for a time in one of
the numerous and intelligent Hawley families,
of which Connecticut has so many, and from
one of which Senator Hawley sprang.

Mrs. Hawley taught me the Bible, and the
poetry of the day, in about equal portions. She
was an old Puritan Presbyterian, and took
everything in the sacred writ as literally as
the most orthodox Scotchman could do; but
she loved at the same time the green meadows
and singing brooks of imagination.

Even when ten years old, I could recite the
first four books of the Old and the first four
books of the New Testament, without a mis
take: and I knew secular poems almost with-

26

out number. Of course, as soon as I began to hear poetry, it made me want to write some. I believe I am not entirely unique in this respect: editors tell me that their mail-bags teem with poetical attempts made by all sorts of people in all sorts of places and on all sorts of subjects.

My first poem, composed when I was eight years old, was as follows:

Oh, what a happy child I am,
    Although I cannot see!
I am resolved that in this world
    Contented I will be.

How many blessings I enjoy
    That other people don't!
So weep or sigh because I'm blind,
    I cannot, nor I won't!

I quote this poem, it is needless to say, not on account of its literary style, or as anything very remarkable, except that it gives an indication of the spirit in which I have taken life throughout all these eighty-three years—of optimism, and of thankfulness because I had as many blessings as I did, rather than of repining because one was left out.

I composed other verses, and always on the subjects nearest me. The fragrance of a rose —the singing of the wind in the trees—the death of a favorite bird—all these inspired me to juvenile effort; and, anxious to hear what others thought of my work, it was not long before I began to free these little stanzas from the leashes of my memory, and let them loose upon my poor dear mother.

She wrote down some of them, and was greatly pleased; she and the good Mrs. Hawley held a literary consultation concerning them. They decided that they were very good, for a girl of that age; and copies were sent to my grandfather.

I now found my first gallant and unqualified admirer. The dear old gentleman wrote a very enthusiastic letter concerning the poor little "pieces", and told my mother that we indeed had a poet in the family, and that if I lived and improved as I ought to do, I would be an honor to them all. "But," he added, cautiously, "you must not *tell* her this, or it will make her proud, and spoil her." And it is due my mother's prudence and good sense, to say, that she never imparted to me anything about my grandfather's encomiums: but he soon saw me, and could not refrain from giving them to me at first hand.

But there was one terrible hunger that afflicted me during all these years: and that was for knowledge—knowledge—knowledge! I felt that there were a million things that I ought to know, and had no means of learning.

If I ever lamented that I was blind, it was through these opening days of girlhood—and that for only one cause: the fact that it debarred me from reading for myself. The amount of literature printed in raised letters for the blind was very limited in those days, and I had been so accustomed to knitting, that my fingers were not adapted to learning how to read by such means, even if alphabets for the blind had been common.

So, night and night again, I have gone to bed drearily, weeping because I could not drink of the waters of knowledge that I knew were surging all around me. I felt at times like a sailor on a great lake of fresh, crystal water, heated and thirsty, but bound hand and foot, so that he could not get to the blesséd relief.

"Dear God, please give me light!" was my prayer, day by day. I did not mean physical light—but mental! I had long been contented to bear the burden of blindness: but my education—my education—how was I to get it? The ordinary schools could do little for me; I was not able to read and educate myself, as many home-students have done; those around had little time to read to me; and I felt as if I were in danger of growing more and more ignorant every day. God help those who thirst for knowledge, and find every way for obtaining it cut off!

Sooner or later, I always rose from my knees feeling that these prayers would be answered. God has always had a way of granting my petitions to Him, some wonderful examples of which I shall give, farther along in this book.

How much better it is to pray, hopefully and with faith, for those things we need, than to fret and complain because we do not already possess them!

CHAPTER IV.—1835.

A THRILLING ANNOUNCEMENT—AN EDUCATION
AT LAST!—ON THE "TIPTOE OF EXPECTATION"
—STARTING FOR SCHOOL—ARRIVAL AT THE
INSTITUTION FOR THE BLIND—A HELPER OF
OPPRESSED GREEKS—AN ACQUAINTANCE OF
LORD BYRON — SCHOOL-LIFE STARTS OFF
WELL.

SO matters ran on, until I was fifteen years
old: and then, one day, something was
told me that brought a thrill of joy and
delight never, never to be forgotten.

"Fanny, arrangements have been made for
you to attend the school for the blind, in New
York."

Only a few words, but what a flood of joy
they admitted to the poor sad little soul that
had so long pined and prayed for knowledge!
God had responded to my prayer, at last—
through His own means, and by His own faithful helpers. Oh, if the founders and sustainers
of such institutions could only know a mil-
lionth part of the joy they cause, they would
feel repaid for their money and their efforts—
again and again!

Of course, I was upon the very tiptoe of expectation—my joy only tempered by the fact

that I should have to leave behind my dear mother, and the friends whom I had learned to love. But the distance was not great, and, so to speak, was becoming less and less all the time, owing to constantly increasing facilities of travel; and I was told that I could return during every vacation, and oftener if I or they should at any time be ill.

The preparations were few and simple: a girl then did not require so many appurtenances when starting for school, as she does now. I was soon ready: and left home on the 3d of March, 1835—searching, as upon my voyage of ten years before, for light—but this time for the mental, instead of the physical, light that should illuminate my mind, and make me happy ever after.

This time, we did not go down the Hudson River, upon a sail-boat: we first journeyed to Norwalk, and there took a steamer for New York.

This, although vastly different from the mammoth sound-steamers of today, served the turn, and brought us through very comfortably: and I was cordially received by Dr. John Denison Russ, who was then Superintendent of the Institution. He was only thirty-four years old, but had already been through an interesting and varied experience. He had settled in New York as a physician after graduating at Yale College, but one year afterward, in 1826, he was so moved with pity at the sufferings of the struggling Greeks, that he went to their aid with a cargo of supplies, from Boston, and remained there three years, during which time he established a hospital at Poros, and conducted it personally for fifteen months.

Returning to New York in 1834, he began at his own expense the instruction of six blind boys; but the same year, was appointed Superintendent of the Institution of which I was happily so soon to become an inmate.

While in Greece, he had been intimately associated with Lord Byron. I shall never forget the thrill of delight, upon meeting some one that had actually known the great poet, whose verses I had already learned to admire. He was full of reminiscences of the poet-patriot, and his recounting of them at times had a great fascination.

Everything started off well: I was a little homesick at first, but frequent letters and new-made friends soon softened that feeling; while fresh facts and ideas were sent thronging every day into my mind.

CHAPTER V.—1835-1836.

SCHOOL-LIFE—THE MONSTER ARITHMETIC AND ITS TERRORS—METAL SLATES—IN LOVE WITH OTHER STUDIES—"DROP INTO POETRY" NOW AND THEN—TEMPTATIONS TO VANITY—A BENEFICIAL "CALL-DOWN" FROM THE SUPERINTENDENT—ALL FOR MY OWN GOOD.

BEHOLD me, now, Miss Fanny Crosby, full-fledged student, in a city school! I assure you, it seemed a great step forward—and upward—to me; one that I had coveted through many years; one whose first joy I can never forget.

Some young ladies creep off to boarding-school unwillingly, and as a solemn duty, and maybe I would do so, were I in their place; but under all these circumstances, the occurrence was a great pleasure in my life, though for a time, as stated in the preceding chapter, I was a little homesick, and longed often to meet again my dear mother and friends.

But the world seems built a good deal like the track of a hurdle-race: you are apparently skipping along at great speed, and all at once you encounter something that must be immediately overcome before you can go a step farther!

33

The first obstacle that I found standing in my way and looming up like a great monster, was Arithmetic. I have never been a very good hater, even when the best material was provided for the purpose; but I found myself an adept at the art of loathing, when it came to the Science of Numbers. The culinary poet who in a fit of dyspepsia exuded the statement

"I loathe, abhor, detest, despise
Those pastry-wrecks, dried apple pies",

had a parodist in me. I could not agree with him concerning the article of food in question, for I like almost everything that a good cook can send to the table; but I *could* say, at that time,

"I loathe, abhor, it makes me sick
To hear the word Arithmetic!"

However, this great foe to my peace of mind had to be conquered, and at it I went, with a vengeance—wishing that every assault would give the Arithmetic a twinge of pain. But no! I was well aware of the fact that the sturdy old creature went right on, without minding me at all, through all the affairs of life, and that we could not do much of anything very long, without consulting him.

The great variety of resources that this terrible study possessed with which to frighten and appal the student, was something terrible to contemplate. Addition and Subtraction went on fairly well, and did not give me so very much trouble; but when the Multiplication

Table made its appearance on the scene, that **was an** entirely different matter. The only alleviation of its miseries was, that it came in a kind of poetical form—a swinging, rhymeless sort of poetry, to be sure—blank verse, I should call it; but that fact, as with many other students, aided me to remember it.

Our toil in Arithmetic was materially aided by metal slates, which had holes in them, with which we could count and realize the numbers as we went on. But I never became an accomplished mathematician, although our school upon the whole was said to be much more advanced in mathematics than students of the same age that could see.

Grammar, Philosophy, Astronomy, and Political Economy followed, among our studies. and with all of these I was in love. Our lessons were given us in the form of lectures and readings, and not many words that came to our ears managed to slip away from us. Indeed, we could not afford to let them do so; for we were closely examined each day by means of questions asked by the teachers, and our progress and standing in the school depended largely upon our ability to remember and recount these lessons.

Noticing the respect and deference paid to our instructors, and realizing how much more personal independence they had, feeling that I wanted to be financially as self-reliant as possible, and most of all wishing to please, comfort, and help my dear mother, I made up my mind to be a teacher, as soon as I could.

Nor did I forget the other friends of my babyhood and youthhood—especially the dear, gallant old grandfather who had so enthusiastically announced that "we had a poet in the family." I composed several little poems from time to time, which, it is no more than fair to say, were received with great favor, by both teachers and fellow-pupils. In the mind of a girl in her "teens", this would naturally produce a little feeling of self-gratulation, and it is possible that in my appearance or behavior, an "air" or two appeared.

Perhaps Mr. Jones, the Superintendent at that time, noticed it: for one morning he came into the school-room, and said,

"I would like to have Fanny Crosby come into my room for a few minutes."

I went, readily enough; supposing that a new ode or other kind of lyric was to be ordered, to the honor of some distinguished person or event: and, perhaps, a little proudly, stood before the Superintendent, at his desk, awaiting his wishes, and hoping that I could find time, among my other duties, to accord to them.

His very first words were a most emphatic surprise, and fully disposed of my theory that I was to write a new poem by request.

"Fanny," he said, "your—your *attempts* at poetry, have brought you into prominence here in the school, and a great deal of flattery has been the result. Shun a flatterer, Fanny, as you would a snake!

Now, I am going to give you some clean

truth, which may hurt just now, but will be of great use one of these days.

"As yet, you know very little about poetry, or, in fact, anything else—compared to what there is to be known. You have almost all of it yet to learn.

"Do not think too much about rhymes, and the praises that come for them. Store your mind with useful knowledge and think more of what you can *be*, than of how you can *appear*.

"The favor and laudation of the world, Fanny, is a very fragile thing upon which to depend. Try to merit the approval of God, and of yourself, as well as that of your fellow-creatures.

"Remember that the very air you breathe— the very food you eat—all the ability or talent that you may develop—come from God.

"Remember that you are always in His presence: and who has any right to be vain for a moment, when standing before the great Owner and Creator of all things?"

He talked to me in this way, kindly but firmly, for perhaps five minutes; and at the end of that time he had convinced me that instead of being the great poet Fanny Crosby, I was really the ignorant young school-girl, who as yet knew scarcely anything whatever.

His words were bomb-shells in the camp of my self-congratulatory thoughts: but they did me an immense amount of good. Something said to me, "He tells the truth, Fanny, and it is all for your own benefit."

Still, the hot tears came to my eyes, as perhaps they would have done to those of any ambitious girl: and I naturally felt much pain and mortification at his words. But a reaction of feeling soon took place: and going around behind his chair, and putting my arms around his neck, I kissed him on the forehead. "You have talked to me as my father would have talked, were he living," I said, "and I thank you for it, over and over again. You have given me a lesson that I might have had to learn through bitter experience, and I shall profit by it."

And I believe I have done so: at least I have tried, through all these eighty-three years. I have done my best to remember that not my poor insignificant self, but the great God above, was entitled to the credit for whatever I could accomplish; and to keep the monster Egotism from coming up between my duty and me.

If in this autobiography, in which I am trying to give a true story of my life, the pronoun of the first person singular number is too often used, the reader must forgive: it is because it is unavoidable, and not because it is in my heart.

CHAPTER VI.—1835-1858.

INCITEMENTS TO AMBITION—GREAT PEOPLE
WHO WERE BLIND—THE IMMORTAL HOMER—
THE KING-POET OSSIAN—JOHN MILTON AND
HIS GENIUS—FRANCIS HUBER, THE NATURAL-
IST—OTHERS WHOSE CAREERS GAVE US EN-
COURAGEMENT.

AMONG the interesting things that we were taught in our Institution, at the very outset, was the fact that scores and hundreds of individuals had achieved fame and fortune, in spite of blindness.

We were told about Homer, the greatest poet of antiquity, who, while traveling to get material for his immortal work, contracted a disease of the eyes, which made him blind forever: but who worked away with renewed ardor; and who, although he died poor, achieved an immortal fame—such as many people would be willing to go blind all their lives, if they could attain.

We were told of Ossian, the Celtic king—who, it is said, was a warrior while he could see, but became a poet after he was stricken with blindness, and sung songs that made him famous forever. Indeed, we were told that

39

his very existence was disputed by some critics: but, for that matter, the same experience had befallen the names of Homer, Virgil, Julius Cæsar, and William Tell. There seemed fully as much reason to believe that he existed, as that he did not; and, as he was, in a manner, one of us, we preferred to take the affirmative of the question.

We were told of Milton, who lost his eyesight from a disease caused by incessant study while he was young: but who, as the light of this world became gradually shut out, grew more and more luminous himself, with sacred lore and imagination. As we heard of the daughters who read to him, and wrote down his grand lines, and who, alas! did not seem always to appreciate the great privilege, many of us girls felt that if we could only have had our sight and assisted such a grand man as that, we would have asked not a single additional pleasure in the world!

Of course we were all proud of Francis Huber, who, notwithstanding the cataracts that grew over his eyes, and blinded him at last, became the historian and biographer of those swift-winged messengers between flower and flower, and garden and hive—the bees. Within his mind he seemed to have constructed a great hive of learning, wherein he sorted, arranged, and made use of the facts that others brought him. He had patience to analyze and compare the different experiments that were made under his direction and that of others— which qualities he might have lacked or never have developed, if he had been "favored" with the power of seeing.

Added to these illustrious names, were given us many who had not climbed to the very top round of fame, but who, although blind, had accomplished more than the average degree of success, in their various callings. Science, mechanics, the "learned professions", and all the miscellaneous pursuits, we found had been ornamented, to a greater or less extent, by the blind.

With this, we were taught that whatever we determined to do, if within the average power of man or woman, we could, with God's help, do—the same as if we had the blessings of sight: and at t we went with a will.

CHAPTER VII.—1835-1858.

VACATIONS—PUPILS WHO ENJOY AND PUPILS
WHO DO NOT ENJOY THEM—AWAITED EACH
TIME BY MOTHER AND SISTERS—CANDY AND
FLOWERS SAVED UP—EXCURSIONS—SWEET
INQUISITIVENESS—AN ENTHUSIASTIC AUDI-
ENCE—SISTERS STILL SPARED.

AMONG pleasant school-memories, the vacations are likely to bear a prominent part. However well a student may love the studies and the discipline of scholastic life, occasional seasons of rest are generally anticipated with keen relish.

I say "generally", because, alas! there are always more or less in every school, who have no pleasant homes to which they can go. Few students are so to be pitied, as are these: others' delight, contrasted with their own loneliness, makes their lot peculiarly hard to bear.

It is one of the numerous blessings which our dear Lord has showered upon me, that I have the most beautiful and winsome of vacation-recollections. Not only my dear and precious mother, but two younger sisters always awaited me with many expressions and other manifestations of delight, and made the occasional home-comings trebly pleasant.

42

Vacation-Delights.

At the coming of vacation, I always has-
tened home as soon as possible : and invariably
found that a royal reception had been reserved
and kept in readiness for "Sister Fan." It
was touching to know that the dear little tots
had been exercising their ingenuity to its fullest extent, to make their "big sister" *feel* the
deliciousness of the home that she could not
see. Sundry bits of candy that had been reso-
lutely saved up for many weeks were slipped
into my hand; flowers of every kind were
brought me, with their fine velvety blossoms
and rich delicate fragrance. Excursions were
planned, to the shadiest of nooks and the most
delightful of forests ; and often to the homes
of dear friends, who received us with unaffect-
ed kindness.

And the questions that I had to answer!
Each little sister had a set entirely of her own,
and all had to be duly considered faithfully
answered, before the little cross-examiners
were satisfied. Of course it was a pleasure to
tell everything to such attentive and apprecia-
tive listeners : and I fully availed myself of the
chance.

Every pupil in the school had to be duly
described; the teachers, with their various peculiarities, all came in for a share of the exami-
nation. Then there were the distinguished
visitors that had favored our Institution with
their calls : these all had to be reviewed in due
course. How often do I remember that small
family-group : the two little sisters snuggling
up to me and clinging to my hands, and my

mother sitting close by, and listening to it all with an indulgent smile, which I could feel though I could not see!

Of course every poem that I had composed since I saw them before, had to be duly recited, and subjected to their criticism. This, however, I am bound to say, was generally favorable, to a degree that bordered on enthusiasm; and it would not have been exactly comfortable for any one rash enough to have intimated to them that their big sister was not the greatest poet of ancient and modern times!

Of course I knew that they would know better, when they became older; but their sweet childish partiality still lingers in my memory, like the fragrance of sweetest flowers.

It has been my blessèd privilege to have these sisters spared to me: one of them, Mrs. Carrie W. Rider, is now my daily companion, and loving protector; while the other, Mrs. Julia Athington, is a near neighbor to us.

I also have several nephews and nieces, at whose homes I am always welcome: and many sweet little vacations are still spent with them.

While nearly all humanity, so far as I have met it, has treated me as a dear sister, there is yet a peculiar and intense pleasure, in feeling that my own near relatives are so loving and congenial.

I am sure the reader will pardon this little digression into family matters: they are a part of me, and necessarily form a portion of my autobiography.

CHAPTER VIII.—1836-1837.

BLIND students, as well as others, have their merry and sportive moods. They can "see" a joke, just as well as if they were not debarred from physical sight; and many are the "games" that they perpetrate upon each other.

It may readily be surmised, then, that our amusements in the Institution were many and varied; and that we indulged in most of the pleasant little plays and other diversions that vary the monotony of "seeing" school-people.

Our socials, musicales, and soirees, were largely frequented by friends from outside, as well as by those of our own number.

Even the cruel process of "hazing" was not always left out of our school-life, although, of course, it was constantly discouraged by the teachers, and the more orderly of the pupils. I suppose we considered ourselves entitled to all the privileges of other schools!

Of course, the Institution being co-educa-
tional, more or less "tender attachments", of
greater or less duration, were formed: and in
these cases, love often laughed at oculars, as
well as locksmiths. The chapel was a favorite
place for short "spooning" seasons, and several
students who could manipulate the piano, had
preconcerted chords which they struck, or
tunes which they played, to let each other
know that they were there, and waiting for
an interview.

Now and then an innocent theft occurred.
One in which I am half ashamed to confess I
was interested, took place one evening in the
garden. The teachers and students had cultivated a fine lot of vegetables: and among them
we knew that there were some luscious watermelons, and our mouths naturally watered for
a share.

All at once, a rumor was circulated that
these melons were to be sold for the benefit
of the school! Whereat, a quiet consternation-
meeting was held, and we decided that, when
it came to what we considered as partly our
own melons, there were different ways of bene-
fiting the Institution. A few of us decided to
have at least one of the largest of the juicy
oblong globes, that very night.

I was only eighteen years old, then, and
may be pardoned for relishing an adventure
that savored somewhat of the madcap variety.
Taking with me into the garden one of the
smaller girls, I concealed her as well as I
could (for it was a moonlight night), told her

to hang on for dear life to a large watermelon that presented itself, and started out to do a little reconnoitering with the senses of touch and hearing.

Ah! a step!—I knew it right well: it was that of Mr. Stevens, the gardener.

"Why, Mr. Stevens!" I exclaimed: "you here?—How do you happen to be walking up and down at this hour of the night?"

"I'm watching out for some of them miserable boys that's tryin' to steal the melons", said the kind but reliable old gentleman. "I'll catch 'em, yet."

"Don't you want me to watch awhile for you, Mr. Stevens?" I inquired, demurely. "You go in and rest: your voice sounds tired. Go and sit down for fifteen minutes, and I'll stay out here, and watch for you. And depend upon it, if a single boy comes, I'll let you know."

Saying this, I led the dear old gentleman indoors, seated him in an easy chair, placed my cool hand on his brow to soothe him a little, and told him to sit there and rest, while I would go on watch for a quarter of an hour. Then I went back to my little stowaway in the garden.

"Take the melon, if you're big enough, and run for our room as soon as you can!" I whispered. She needed only one set of directions; and girl and melon were soon quite a distance away.

At the end of the fifteen minutes, I went back to Mr. Stevens, and told him that not a boy had been near; and, having by this time enjoyed a good rest and a quiet little nap, he went back to his vigil, first thanking me for my help.

When I returned to the room, the dissected fruit was all ready to be still further dissected: and we enjoyed it all the better for the mild little adventure.

A few years afterward, I told the Superintendent about it, and we enjoyed a hearty laugh together over the incident. To think how you blind children were all the while getting the start of us 'seeing' people!" he chuckled. As for good Mr. Stevens, the gardener, he had then gone on where, it is to be hoped, wicked boys and girls do not molest, and where watermelons would not be particularly refreshing.

LATEST PHOTOGRAPH.

CHAPTER IX.—1836-1842.

"STRENUOUS" WORK—HOW A BLIND PERSON CAN TOIL, INTELLECTUALLY—BECOME ONE OF THE TEACHERS—THE "WITCHING SPRITE" OF POETRY—FORBIDDEN TO COMPOSE ANY POETRY FOR THREE MONTHS—PHRENOLOGY TO THE RESCUE!

I THINK it may be said truly that I toiled night and day. "How can a blind person work intellectually?"—do you ask? Better perhaps than one that can see. It is not necessary for us to record in writing as we go along, everything we think and accomplish: we can put it upon the tablets of memory, and copy it down or have it copied as we get opportunity. Memory, when cultivated, grows a wonderful treasure-house of ripened grain.

I do not want to boast of my progress; but as I look back over the past, it gives me a little feeling of pride to be able to say that at the rather early age of twenty-two, I was considered competent to teach Grammar, Rhetoric, and Ancient and Modern History; and became one of the regular instructors of the Institution.

What a pleasure it then was, to feel that I was imparting to others the same blessings of knowledge for which I had longed, through so many weary days and nights!

While preparing for this position, there was still one restless, witching little sprite that kept creeping up to me by night and day, and inviting me to take trips with her into the unknown; and the name of that sprite was Poetry. She was ever tugging away at my hands, or my hair, or my heartstrings, and whispering, "Sister Fanny, come with me."

The faithful Superintendent seemed in doubt whether to encourage me in my poetical pursuits or not. He finally talked to me a long while on the subject, said there were a great many people who wrote rhymes because they were poetry-lovers rather than poets, and finally gently but firmly forbade my producing any more of the dangerous article, for three months.

I did not understand his object in doing this; but suppose now that it was to see if a certain amount of abstinence would not cure me of the habit, or disease, whichever he considered it.

I did not like it, "a little bit"; but, feeling that the good Superintendent knew what was best for me, I acquiesced, and religiously avoided a rhyme as I would the measles.

It was one of the trials of my life: for, whether or not I would "lisp in numbers", they inevitably "came."

Singularly enough I soon gained my little triumph in the matter; for about this time we had a visit from Dr. George Combe, a distinguished phrenologist, of Scotland. Dr. Combe had found himself a convert to the science, in Edinburgh, while Spurzheim was there; and had published several works on the subject.

When he came to America, he "took in" our school, among the other sights; and several of us had the honor of feeling the touch of his learned hand upon our throbbing, and, I trust, not distended heads.

Just before he came to me, he examined the phrenological organs of one of our boy-pupils. "Why, here is a splendid mathematician!" he exclaimed. "He could do anything in mathematics!" And the Doctor was right; for this little fellow was almost another Zera Colburn. He could already do a great many wonderful things: for instance, he could listen to two persons talking to him at the same time, and then, while singing a song, could inform both of them the number of seconds they were old— they of course first giving him the years, weeks, and months. (I used to notice, by the way, that very few ladies availed themselves of the offered courtesy.)

When I heard the boy praised, and reflected on those wonderful things he could do, I was almost envious, and wondered why the good Lord could not have given *me* a few of the figures and groups of figures that seemed to line every portion of his brain. I trembled when my turn came to have the head examined, and felt a wild impulse to run. Dr. Combe said,

"Why! here is a poet! Give her every advantage that she can have; let her hear the

best books and converse with the best writers ,
and she will make her mark in the world."

The next morning our Superintendent sent
for me to come to his room. "Fanny," he exclaimed, "you may write all the poetry you want
to." From that time, the advice of Dr. Combe
was followed: I was prompted to write poetry,
was taught how lines should rhyme, and in
every way encouraged. And I am bound to
say that for a great part of this favorable decision as regarded the wooing of my muse, I
was indebted to Phrenology, and the good Dr.
Combe.

DR. COMBE'S ENDORSEMENT IS OF BENEFIT—
THE "POET LAUREATE" OF THE INSTITUTION—
TAUGHT HOW TO WRITE POETRY—HAMILTON
MURRAY'S AID—A REUNION AFTER SIXTY-
FIVE YEARS' ABSENCE.

FROM the time that good Dr. Combe proclaimed me a poet, I was so considered by my teachers and associates; and they "knew then that they had known the fact from the first." But it takes a certain amount of outside endorsement to make even our best and nearest friends appreciate us; and this I had heretofore lacked. It was for the famous Scotch Phrenologist to set me, if I can say it without being suspected of a pun, upon my poetical feet.

I was now, I think it may be said without vanity, considered as the poet laureate of our Institution; and the teachers evidently determined to make a first-class writer of me, if cultivation could do it. I was taught all the intricacies of verse, until I began to wonder that the subject which I had considered as a very simple, easy sort of thing, had so many complications. I was taught to analyze, to parse, to scan, to write in different measures; and began to worry lest I should disappoint the high expectations that the phrenologist had raised.

Among the most potential aids I received at the time, was that from a gentleman named Hamilton Murray. Mr. Murray claimed that he could not write poetry, but could teach others how to do so; and as pupils in that branch of study were not numerous, he seemed to take especial pleasure in giving me prosodical instruction. He had a poetic temperament, and a fine rich voice: and hour after hour he would read me some of the grandest poems he could find in English literature.

This, as you may readily imagine, was a luxurious feast: and a benefit. Mr. Murray also encouraged me to imitate, as nearly as I could, the different poetical masters of that day—as Bryant, Willis, etc. He pointed out, with much delicacy, the different defects in my literary style, and tried his best to remove them. With rare faithfulness, and with much kindness, considering that his pupil was not a rich man's daughter, but a poor blind girl just starting in life, he toiled for my benefit; and though I could not pay him in money, he had my heartfelt gratitude. He has long walked the streets of the great Tuneful City: and I hope some day to meet him there, grasp him by the hand, and thank him once more.

Not long ago, I had the pleasure of meeting his nephew, Mr. Bronson Murray, of New York: whom I had also known at that time. He was of about my own age, and from him I had always received the most gentle and manly courtesies. We now met again for the first time in sixty-five years : and the reminiscences that were awakened, may be readily imagined. Seldom have I enjoyed a visit so much.

How do these old friendships draw compound interest, as the years go on! And what a grand treat it will be, in the next world, to meet all those whom we have known and loved here, and talk over the events of the past!

MUSICAL DIVERSIONS FOR THE BLIND—NEIGH-
BORLY CALLS—SOIREES—WILLIAM CULLEN
BRYANT VISITS US—HIS KINDNESS TO THE
GIRL-POET—TWO VISITS WITH HORACE GREE-
LEY—SHOWING PEOPLE ABOUT THE INSTITU-
TION—HOW THE BLIND "FIND THE WAY TO
THEIR MOUTHS."

WE had fine music in our school; for
as is well known, some of the best
musicians in the world come from
among the blind. Indeed, an aug-
mented delicacy of hearing generally com-
pensates for loss of sight. We often had
"musical soirees", and invited our neighbors
in the city: and one evening we were electri-
fied by the intelligence that the great William
Cullen Bryant was coming as one of our
guests!

Bryant was at that time the best-known
American poet. Longfellow had not then written the books upon which hang most of his
fame; Whittier was yet known rather as an
Anti-Slavery agitator than as a writer of verse;
and Willis, though a brilliant author and trav-
eler, was obliged to yield to his older and more
finished contemporary.

Bryant had composed at twenty-three his "Thanatopsis", the sweetest apology for Death in any language (I wonder if that was the reason Death finally spared him so long?). He had with his other poems attracted the attention and commanded the admiration of the world; had traveled extensively in Europe; and had now (1843) settled down for a time in editorial work.

As was the case almost wherever he went, he was obliged to hold a little impromptu reception at our soiree; and among those that were introduced to him, was poor little timid I, who had very little hope that he would greet me otherwise than conventionally, and as a stranger of whom he had never heard before.

To my surprise, however, he gave me a warm grasp of the hand, commented upon my poor little rhythmical efforts, commended them in a tone that I felt to be sincere, and told me to go on bravely and determinedly with my work. He never knew how much good he did, by those few words, to the young girl that had hardly hoped to touch the hem of his proud robe of poetic genius!

At a children's party on New Year's, 1844, I met for the first time Horace Greeley. He was then only thirty-three years old; had come to New York a journeyman printer, and fought his way into recognition. He had already founded the "Tribune", and, of course, to meet him was an event.

But I must say that I at first was disappointed in him: perhaps I expected too much. "Is *that* the great Horace Greeley?" I pondered, after hearing him talk. I had never been able to read any of his editorials, but concluded, in my inexperience, that if they were no more brilliant than his conversation, the world was making a queer mistake in honoring him.

I did not understand, at that time, as I have learned since, that great men have widely varying moods, and that they are at one time silently gathering up that which at another they dispense so lavishly.

The following summer I happened to meet him at the house of a mutual friend; and a more charming and intelligent conversationalist, I never heard. History, literature, social ethics, political economy—all subjects—seemed perfectly natural and easy to him; and no one else wished to talk, so long as *he* could be kept talking.

Of course, being human, I did not admire him one whit the less, when he insisted on my reciting to him some of my little poems, praised them, and invited me to write for his paper!

I hardly knew whether I walked or flew to my room that night: I was so proud at having been recognized as a poet by such a great genius as Horace Greeley!

On another occasion, during that same year, I remember feeling equally proud; and that was when I heard that my gallant old grandfather, who had been so enthusiastic in praising my juvenile abilities and so anxious that I should not be spoiled, wrote that he walked four miles to get a paper that had in it a poem written by me, and felt well paid for his trouble!

Our little Institution of one hundred and fifty students was under State control and patronage, and the Government naturally took much interest in it, and sent us as many interested visitors as it could. Institutions for the benefit of the blind were not so common as they are now, and we were quite objects of curiosity. The visitors, having read my poems in the different papers, where they had been published and republished, sometimes asked to be shown about the place by me. It was, in a manner, the blind leading those that were not blind; but I knew every inch of the establishment, almost as well as if I could see.

For a time, this piloting was a pleasant novelty; but, of course, it finally grew a little irksome to answer the same questions again and again, and I became quite willing to depute the pleasure to others. One bright boy, who had been guiding a large party of ladies and gentlemen through the rooms and halls, reported that they had asked him as they entered the dining-room, how blind people managed to find the way to their mouths while eating. "What did you tell them?" we inquired. "I informed them," said the blind boy, gravely, "that we hitched one end of a string to the leg of our chair, and the other to our tongue; and by that means managed to prevent the victuals losing their way."

The teachers gently reproved him; but I had opportunity to know, that they laughed over the queer little episode, many times, afterward.

CHAPTER XII.—1843.

ONE of the most enjoyable trips I ever took in connection with our Institution for the Blind, was—not in a daintily upholstered palace car—not in a finely appointed and swiftly gliding ocean-steamship—not in an exquisitely poised and jauntily driven mountain coach—but—strange to say!—upon a canal-boat.

Railroads were not bewilderingly plenty, in those days, as they are now; and it had not occurred to anybody that it would be desirable to build one along the valley of the Mohawk River, and then away off still westward—westward—to Buffalo—to Chicago—to the very Pacific Ocean itself! If any one had told us that such a thing would happen, "one of these days", we would have considered him as one of the blind who was trying to lead the blind.

But, largely through the energy and perseverance of Governor DeWitt Clinton, an artificial river had been stretched from the Hudson to Lake Erie; and few that are living now, can comprehend what a convenience and help to the country was this great highway of waves. Miniature ships—propelled by horses and mules, carrying great boat-loads of merchandise up and down through the country, may still be seen, by passengers on the New York Central Railroad trains, from the windows of its fast-flying coaches; and they think little of them.

But in those days they were among the principal commercial institutions of the country. When the Erie Canal was opened, Governor Clinton, who had dug the first spadeful of earth in the construction of the giant channel, was greeted, on his first trip, all along the line, with the ringing of bells, and the firing of cannon, and more or less eloquent speeches wherever he would stop long enough to hear them. It would be interesting if one could know how many people thronged the banks of the Erie Canal, during those days of triumph, to see Governor Clinton go past!

One who from curiosity or other reason visits the crafts employed nowadays, can form little idea of the elegance with which passenger, or "packet" boats were fitted up, in those days. Many people preferred traveling in them, even when on business, to using stage-coach or carriage; and a long boat-ride, through the finest of scenery, among pleasant people, without jolting, and surrounded with the comforts of every-day life—was not half unenjoyable.

So we had, as it were, our "private car", all to ourselves; and were not long in taking possession of, and appropriating it. The crew, consisting of captain, driver, and maid, met us rather coldly, when we came on board, and acted as if they were afraid of us; but they soon found out, as they expressed it, that we'd "do." They explained, after getting acquainted, that they had supposed we would be a quiet, sad, sober, melancholy lot of people, moping about with grief on our faces, the constant burden of whose song was, "I'm blind, oh, I'm blind."

Without wishing to recommend too highly the vivacity of my companions and myself, I may say, that they revised their opinions, within about five minutes after we got on board. They found that we were inclined to enjoy life in every way that solid instruction and innocent amusement could give. It was not long before we knew our temporary aquatic guardians "as well as if we'd been through 'em with a lantern", as the captain luminously expressed it. We were all over the boat in a jiffy, and knew every nook and corner of it before the expedition started. "Well, you're a rum lot, Miss Crosby", the Captain confided to me, in one of our first conversations: "an' it's the jolliest crew I ever shipped. To tell the truth, I dreaded you, an' expected to strike a sort of fun'ral percession, the hull length of the big ditch; but I guess it's goin' to be a circis, all the way, an' a good one."

It was not a "circis" all the way, for there came times when we were very sober, staid, and circumspect; but we could not resist the exhilarating air of the hill-regions through which we passed, or the genial sunshine, or the smell of the flowers, or the cheery hail of boatmen and passengers whom we met along the moist way. We soon learned the construction of the locks, and how it was that our boat ran into the large basin and waited till that was filled or emptied, as the case might demand, in order to get us on the level required; and after the novelty of that was over, we often ran ahead on the tow-path, accompanied by one of our "seeing" teachers, and had a nice little bit of exercise before our steady-going craft overtook us.

We stopped at all towns of any size on the way, such as Schenectady, Rome, Utica, Syracuse, Rochester, as well as many others, and gave entertainments. I may say, without exaggeration, that these affairs were the events of the evening, if not of the week and month, in the vicinity where we appeared.

The Mayor would generally preside; and give us as fine a speech of welcome as he had time to prepare. The Common Council, or Board of Aldermen, and other distinguished people, were very likely also to sit upon the platform; while hundreds if not thousands of the citizen-rank-and-file were down in front.

What with our singing, addresses, descriptions of our school, recitations, and such oratorical and musical help as we managed to borrow from local talent, we flattered ourselves that we made a pretty good "show", as we used playfully to call it; and we were always overwhelmed with praises, and invitations to "come again."

Besides this, we generally netted a snug little sum for the Institution: although the main object of the excursion was the rousing of public interest in our educational work.

After a day or two of rest in a town, meeting kind friends, partaking of splendid hospitality, encouraging sightless people who heard of and came to us from all directions—we would set sail again, and start for the next "stand"—delighted to get back again to our dear old canal-boat — containing, as Dr. Holmes used to say, "many of the pleasures of navigation, with none of its perils."

And so we went on and on—till at last Buffalo was reached, and after arriving there we were not long in making a pilgrimage to the great Niagara Falls.

CHAPTER XIII.—1843.

WHEN our canal-party had left its boat-home and extended its pil grimage to the great Niagara Falls, we felt as if one of the great days of our life had come.

"But what could *you* see of the Falls?" some one asks. Much more than you would suppose, dear friend! Seeing is not all done with the optical organs.

Besides, we had in our school learned all about this gigantic plunge of four great lakes one hundred and sixty-four feet, into the rocky gulfs below; we had seen it over and over again with our imaginations; and knew well what was going on (or, rather, off) before us.

As we stood upon Goat Island, and one of our teachers described the Horseshoe Falls and other famous localities in his view, I could almost fancy I heard the morning stars singing together, and the sons of God shouting for joy!

I could imagine those great rocks that had stood for ages, while the river-billows went sweeping over them night and day, summer and winter, through century after century.

I could at that time perceive enough of light and color (although as ever unable to distinguish objects), to appreciate somewhat the opulence of hue that leaped and flowed around us; though of late years, even that power has departed from me, and if I should stand upon the borders of that great tossing precipice to-day, even in the midst of the most brilliant sunshine, I could not get even a fragment of the wonderful chromatic feast.

But I could still hear the trumpet-voice of this king of cataracts, proclaiming the power of the Almighty hand; I could feel the fresh breezes that spring from the bosom of the whirling waters; I could (sweetest thought of all) enjoy the enjoyment of my friends who could see, and listen to their animated descriptions.

Indeed, I sometimes think that blind people see more than their friends who have the power of vision: for they get descriptions from various points of view, that it is not considered necessary to give to those who can look for themselves.

We wandered all about the different localities, and had everything described to us, until we felt as if we knew the place by heart. We stood upon the great Table Rock—then one of the principal curiosities of the "Falls", but now fallen from its high estate into the gulf below;

we lingered by the whirlpool, and imagined ourselves drawn into that mighty vortex. We walked up and down through the streets of the little village, and wondered what our sensations would be if we lived there with that continual peal of thunder in our ears.

Many and interesting incidents were related to us by "the oldest inhabitants"—all of whom, alas! are now in the grave—with the mammoth cataract singing their requiem.

Among the other things told us, was the way "Goat Island" happened to be named. It was after one poor old animal that belonged to a Mr. John Stedman, as long ago as 1779. He placed the poor old fellow there in the summer of that year, and left him alone for a while when autumn came, intending to row over and get him (there was no bridge then) "before snow flew." But, alas, for the poor goat!—winter set in early that year, navigation to and from the main shore was impossible, and the animal died of starvation or exposure—taking his pay for the sacrifice in giving his name, or the name of his species, for centuries to come, to the world-renowned island. It has been given other titles temporarily, and was very prettily marked on one of the maps, "Iris Island"; but people generally have always been loyal to the poor old quadruped who died there in the winter of 1779-80, and continue to call it Goat Island.

They told us so many stories of accidents, rescues, suicides, and other incidents almost as wonderful as the Falls themselves, that we were well-nigh bewildered; and it took many weeks of our quiet and systematic school-life in New York to straighten everything out in our minds. It required much longer for us to satisfy all the curiosity of those of our school-mates who had not been so fortunate as to go with us. There was no envy expressed—only delight that we were able to enjoy so much, and genuine pleasure that they could partici-pate, even if indirectly, in the pleasures of the trip.

CHAPTER XIV.—1844-1847.

OFF TO THE NATIONAL CAPITAL AND CAPITOL—
BEFORE THE SENATE AND HOUSE OF REPRE-
SENTATIVES—MEET AND HEAR JOHN QUINCY
ADAMS—JAMES BUCHANAN—ANDREW JOHN-
SON—STEPHEN A. DOUGLAS—WILLIAM L.
DAYTON—JOHN P. HALE—RUFUS CHOATE—
R. H. BAYARD—ROBERT J. WALKER—OTHER
FAMOUS MEN IN THE AUDIENCE.

IN January, 1844, a party of us went to Washington, in order to awaken public attention in favor of the blind. We were asked to appear before the Senate and House of Representatives gathered in joint session: and here, in a poetical address which I was invited to give them, I had one of the most distinguished audiences of my life.

You may well imagine that it was with some trepidation that a young woman still in her twenties, appeared before Congress: I have been told that I was the first and last poet ever invited to speak, or to recite his or her own productions before the great National Assembly. But I nerved myself to the task, and did as well as I could; and had the pleasure of receiving an enthusiastic encore.

Greatest of all who were present on that

day, was John Quincy Adams. He was seventy-six years old, and had nearly all his life occupied some prominent office in the service of our country. He had been President of United States eighteen years before; and was now in his old age winning new laurels as a most worthy Representative in the Lower House of Congress.

During our stay in Washington I had the pleasure of hearing his speech on the subject of the Smithsonian Institute, and had the pleasure of a friendly greeting from him, and a clasp of his hand.

There was also a man in the audience whose father had emigrated from Ireland seventy-one years before, and whose mother was the daughter of a Pennsylvania farmer. This man had worked his way up, through various offices, until he was now United States Senator; and sixteen years afterwards he was elected President. His name was James Buchanan.

There was one comparatively young man, thirty-nine years of age: who had already commenced a unique career. As a tailor's apprentice, unable to read or write, he had sat upon his bench, sewing up seams, while listening to books read aloud by a gentleman who used to come into the shop and read, in order to improve the minds of the workmen: and among the selections, some public speeches were reproduced, which had fired the young man's natural talent. He became ambitious, learned to read, and, marrying before he was of age, was taught to write, by his wife. He had been elected alderman of the little Tennessee town in which he settled, then mayor, then was sent to the legislature, and finally to Congress.

This tailor's apprentice-boy, Andrew Johnson, was yet to be a United States senator, a governor of his state, a vice-president, and finally by the death of the great Lincoln, President of United States. After a stormy administration, he was to retire to his home in Tennessee, to be sent to Washington once more as United States senator, and to die before he had fully entered upon his new political career.

There was also Hannibal Hamlin, who, only thirteen years afterwards, was to be elected Vice-President on the same ticket that gave the Presidency to Lincoln; and who, after that term expired, lived many years in public life.

Stephen A. Douglas was also present. He was then thirty-one years old, being only forty-eight when he died, just after his defeat by Abraham Lincoln, in his canvass for the Presidency. His career was already a most promising one, and "The Little Giant", as he was called, was even then making his mark.

William L. Dayton, of New Jersey, was there: he was to run in 1856 for the Vice-Presidency, and be defeated, as was the head of the Republican ticket, John C. Fremont.

John P. Hale, of New Hampshire, who in 1852 ran for the Presidency on the Free Soil ticket, was also present on this occasion, being then a member of the Lower House of Congress.

Rufus Choate, the celebrated lawyer, was also there, serving out the unexpired term of Daniel Webster, who died soon after its beginning. Mr. Choate, it is said, did not feel at home in Congress, and was at his best when pleading at the bar.

Others who had at that time gained some prominence, and who afterwards achieved national and in some cases international renown, were R. H. Bayard, a Senator from Delaware; Robert J. Walker, from Mississippi; John J. Crittenden, of Kentucky, and Thomas H. Benton ("Old Bullion"), of Missouri.

There were in the House-portion of my audience, besides those already mentioned, Robert C. Winthrop, of Massachusetts; Hamilton Fish and Preston King, of New York; Henry A. Wise, of Virginia; Howell Cobb, of Georgia; John Slidell, of Louisiana; Robert Dale Owen, of Indiana, and "Long John" Wentworth, of Illinois.

Little did I think that there also sat before me, a man who was one day to be President of a Southern Confederacy, and one of the principal figures in a titanic war between the North and South. This was Jefferson Davis, only three months older than Johnson, and destined to live four years longer than he—dying in 1879.

There also sat before me, and did me the honor of listening, Alexander Stephens—thirty-five years old, who was destined to be Vice-President of the Confederacy, of which Jefferson Davis was President.

There were also in the audience that day,
Joshua R. Giddings, a prominent Pennsyl-
vania statesman; R. M. T. Hunter, of Virginia;
William L. Yancey, of Alabama; Robert
Toombs, of Georgia; and others who have
since become more or less famous.

Added to these, were many others, perhaps
equal to their more fortunate brothers who
achieved celebrity, but who were debarred
from it, maybe by circumstances beyond their
control, or that of any one except Him who
holds the failure and success of humanity
within His all-powerful hand.

In April, 1847, we went to Washington
again, and I once more had the privilege of
appearing before Congress. Among the
auditors on that occasion, were most of those
above-mentioned, and in addition were several
others who have since achieved additional
fame.

While I could not see these brilliant men,
I could feel their kindness, their appreciation,
and their sympathy; I was introduced to many
of them, and have followed with interest their
course through life.

I naturally many times think about them,
although now most if not all of them are dead
and gone, and wonder how they could have
been so kind as to listen to a young woman in
her twenties, and to treat her with so much
consideration. They were all intensely ambitious, although, mostly, obscure; and in the
midst of their strenuous public life, they
showed, by this considerate treatment of their

blind visitors, that "one touch of nature makes the whole world kin."

While in Washington we visited a great many historical places, and felt the thrill of the great deeds that had been performed there. If we could not see with the eye those objects of interest, we could with the imagination: which, like other faculties, grows stronger the more it is used.

CHAPTER XV.—1844-1897.

COLLECT POEMS AND PUBLISH A BOOK—"THE
BLIND GIRL AND OTHER POEMS"—MY "DE-
CLINING HEALTH"—DELIVERING A POEM BE-
FORE THE NEW JERSEY LEGISLATURE—AN-
OTHER VOLUME, "MONTEREY AND OTHER
POEMS"—MY "DECLINING YEARS" FIFTY-TWO
YEARS AGO—STILL ANOTHER BOOK, "A
WREATH OF COLUMBIA'S FLOWERS"—PROSE
STORIES—"BELLS AT EVENING."

IN 1844, I was induced to collect a number
of my poems, for the purpose of publishing them in a volume.

The idea seemed to me at first pre-
sumptuous!—the thought of being styled an
"author" was almost too much for my nerves.
But after awhile, the matter was arranged—
partly in spite of me, and partly in accordance
with my gradually growing desires: and the
book was finally published, by the firm of
Wiley & Putnam, who then occupied offices
at 161 Broadway.

The name of this book, which contained 160
pages—exactly the same number as this
story of my life—was mentioned, on the title-
page, as "The Blind Girl and Other Poems:

By Frances Jane Crosby, a Pupil at the New York Institution for the Blind " (It will be noticed that my original name, Frances Jane, was soon modified into the more diminutive and more easily wielded one, of Fanny.) Upon the title-page were these lines from Milton:

"—who best
Bears his mild yoke, they serve him best; his
      state
Is kingly."

The Preface was written by Hamilton Murray, a good friend of mine, mentioned elsewhere in this book, and bespoke in eloquent terms the favor of a discriminating public. It traced my career thus far, such as it was, vouched for the fact that all the compositions were "the unaided productions of the authoress", apologized for some peculiarities of punctuation which might, it thought, have served the purpose better if I could only have seen, so as to attend to it myself—and stated that my "declining health" rendered its financial avails all the more important. So strange are the decrees of the Master of the Universe!—I have outlived my good friend for thirty-five years, and, although then in delicate health, do not consider myself so at present.

After a dedication in rhyme to the officers of the Institution, the first poem was the one that gave its title to the book—"The Blind Girl." It commenced with the following lines, which were to some extent descriptive of my own birthplace,

"Her home was near an ancient wood,
Where many an oak gigantic stood,
And fragrant flowers of lovely hue
In that sequestered valley grew";

and went on for several lines to picture that little home, as well as I could do it with my imagination. The heroine of the poem was "Anna"; she lost her mother at an early age, and, in addition to the physical affliction that had fallen upon her, a mental blindness gradually came. Just as she was yielding to despair, a stranger appeared, who conducted her to our "home erected for the blind"— where she, happily, received "Education's glorious light."

This poem was suggested by an incident that occurred while we were upon one of our trips to the interior of New York State.

The next poem was "The Rise and Progress of the New York Institution for the Blind", and contained a short history of its career. Then followed "Dedication of the Chapel", then an "Address", delivered to the Senate of New York, upon the occasion of its visiting our Institution; and then "The Blind Girl's Lament", and "The Desolate."

My next poem in the book was of a patriotic nature, and was "To the Heroes of Bunker Hill." Then followed "Reflections on the Closing year" (1843), "The Captive", "Thoughts at Midnight", etc., etc.

My first hymn **was** published in this book.

It was entitled "An Evening Hymn", and is printed on another page.

There was also one that had been delivered before the Governor, Council, and Assembly of the State of New Jersey, Jan. 29, 1844; and two that were recited at several exhibitions on our tours in August, 1842.

In 1851, another volume was published— this one by R. Craighead, of 112 Fulton Street. It was entitled "Monterey and Other Poems". and had for its motto these lines from Milton:

"As the wakeful bird
Sings darkling, and in shadiest covert hid
Tunes her nocturnal note."

This motto, it may be needless to say, was selected by one of my friends, and not myself. In the Preface of this book I spoke of my continued bad health, and my "declining years": little thinking that I would be issuing my autobiography a little matter of *fifty-two years afterward*. I was under a feeling of sadness and depression at this time, but, happily, the good Lord at last gave me the power to shake it off and commence life with new zest and courage.

This book had in it some of the echoes of the war between United States and Mexico, which had recently been in progress. It contained, besides the initial poem, lines on the death of Maj. Ringgold, Col. Clay, and Gen. Taylor, who had been elevated to the Presidency on account of his being one of the heroes of this same Mexican War.

Other Poems.

In 1858 came another book, "A Wreath of Columbia's Flowers"—published by H. Dayton, at 107 Nassau Street.

This work was partly in prose: commencing with a story, "The Mountain Chief; or, the Home of Medora." "Annie Herbert" was another; "Philip Synclare; or, the Traitor's Reward", and "Magerie; or, the Sibyl of the Revolution" were additional ones.

These books all had a good sale, but are now out of print.

In 1897, appeared "Bells at Evening and Other Verses", with a short biographical sketch by Rev. Robert Lowry, the famous composer. This book was issued for me, by the Biglow & Main Company, New York: who have also published many of my hymns, and with whom I have maintained most cordial and even affectionate relations, for many years past.

WHEN we were at Oswego, upon the canal-trip mentioned in a previous chapter, a lady came to us, bringing a blind boy, just about to enter the years of manhood. I little thought, then, that my destiny would be indissolubly linked with his own.

His name was Alexander Van Alstyne. The mother appealed to me in particular, as I was one of the teachers, although, it must be confessed, young for such a position, and asked me to take her "boy" especially under my personal charge, and see that no harm came to him.

I consented, perhaps rather thoughtlessly · but the responsibility was fated to have more important results than I supposed.

He entered the Institution in 1844, and was in several of my classes during the four years he remained with us. In 1848 he graduated, and then went to Union College, Schenectady,

WIFE AND HUSBAND.

where he studied Greek, Latin, and Theology.

Although he became well grounded in general studies, and, indeed, distinguished himself by his scholarship, his natural profession was Music, and he became a most accomplished performer, teacher, and composer—being fully conversant with the works of the old masters. He felt that all the mental discipline that he could procure in general studies, would enrich his mind, and enable him to succeed better in his own vocation: and results proved the truth of that theory.

In 1855, he came back to our Institution for the Blind, and for two years was a teacher there, and in 1858, we were married.

We found in each other not only perfect congeniality, but sympathy in our pursuits: neither of us interfered with the other's professional career. Each of us (as is not always the case) could sympathize with the other's occupation, without rivalry or interference. He set several of my hymns to music: but his taste was mostly for the wordless melodies of the classics. He insisted that my literary name should remain as it was: I yielded to his desire, and although really Mrs. Van Alstyne, have always written under the name of Fanny Crosby, except when using soubriquets.

His father, Wells Van Alstyne, came from the banks of the Rhine, while still young, bringing his wife with him. He was an engineer by profession, and bore a prominent part in the construction of the Welland Canal.

For many years my husband taught music,

and proved himself a brilliant instructor. He was proficient upon the piano and the cornet —and long occupied the position of organist in one of the city churches of New York.

He was not only a musician, but a philosopher, and a deep student of human nature. He delighted in bringing out latent musical talent, wherever he could find it. He often taught pupils free, in cases where they were not able to pay.

"Van", as everybody who knew him affectionately called him, was always an inspiration in any company in which he was present, with his ready wit, his winning magnetism, and his cheery ways. It has been told me by those who could see, that when he was at the organ or piano, his face bore the happiest expression of any they had ever witnessed in like circumstances. He had his faults—and so have I mine —and as I suppose have all of us frail mortals: but notwithstanding these, we loved each other to the last. We were long spared bereavement: but he was taken sick in 1901, with asthma, and after a long illness, died on June 18th, 1902, of a complication of diseases.

He was buried in Brooklyn, not far from where we first established our little home, soon after marriage: and there, though I cannot see the mound under which he rests, I can touch the turf with my hands, and try to make his spirit feel that I am constantly lamenting his temporary loss.

CHAPTER XVII.—1845.

THE BLIND NOT SO EASILY DECEIVED—WAYS TO
ASCERTAIN WHAT IS "GOING ON"—LOVE-MAK-
ING BEFORE THE BLIND NOT ALWAYS SAFE—
WIRELESS TELEGRAPHY OF THE MIND, HEART,
AND SOUL—THE BLIND CHILD FROM NEW
JERSEY—GRIEVES FOR HIS GRANDMOTHER
—ACTING THE PART OF THE GOOD OLD LADY
—THE LITTLE BOY HAPPY.

ALTHOUGH they cannot see what is going on around them, yet the blind are
not by any means so easily duped,
as many suppose: for there are numerous ways in which they can know what is "doing", almost as well as if they could witness
it with good eyes, under the clear light of a
noonday sun. Little by-plays often take place
near me, the existence of which I am not supposed to know: but of which, in almost every
detail, I am fully aware.

Even surreptitious love-making has been
attempted in my presence, the parties trusting
to my physical blindness to serve as a wall
with which to hide themselves: but I have
been able, a few times, to laughingly inform
these amiable but misguided people, that I was,
really, an involuntary spectator of their actions.

There are many ways in which we perceive. Sound, for instance, has delicate modifications and variations, that no one who has no opportunity for making a study of them would suspect. Slight jarrings, and the sudden changing of currents of air, all have their effect upon most blind people.

Then there is that indescribable wireless telegraphy of the mind, heart, and soul—of which every one has more or less—whether perceived and utilized or not: and this the blind generally cultivate and employ to its utmost capacity.

Sometimes, however, especially with the very young, a certain amount of deceit can be successfully practiced. Occasionally it is for their own good, as in the following case:

In 1845, a little blind boy, six years old, was sent to us from a New Jersey town. Coming from a home where he had naturally been petted by every member of the family, into strange and more austere surroundings, he was of course sad and homesick, and cried all day and all night—when he was awake—for his old home and those whom he knew and loved there.

The Superintendent informed me, one day, that we should probably have to send him back again. "He keeps calling all the time for those he has left behind him, and especially for his grandmother. If the good lady could come once a week, or so, and talk with him a while, it would no doubt make him contented: but she writes that she is unable to do so."

84

Playing Grandmother.

It occurred to me that a little harmless de-
ception would not be out of place here: and
I made up my mind to act the part of grandmother, and visit the poor little fellow two or
three times per week. I wrote to the good old
lady, told her the circumstances, and what I
wished to do, and asked her for all the information that she could give me, which would
help in the impersonating.

She willingly responded, and, although only
twenty-five years of age, I carefully "made
up", in voice, manner, and conversational material, for the part of a grandmother of his own
flesh and blood.

The next time I heard him calling for her,
I rushed into the room, and exclaimed, "My
dear little boy, Grandma has come! She wanted to see you so bad, she couldn't stay away
another minute!"

"O Grandma, Grandma, Grandma!" the
poor little fellow shouted, rushing into my
arms, sobbing, meanwhile, with joy. "I
thought you would *never* come!" He kissed
me affectionately, not noticing, in his haste,
the eradication of sundry wrinkles that he
must have left on the dear old lady's face when
he came away from home; and as soon as he
was calm, he made an elaborate series of in-
quiries that put my memory and ingenuity to
the fullest test. Not only the human friends
and relatives, but every hen and chicken that
he had left on the home-farm, had to be ac-
counted-for. The recent behavior of several
lambs, cats, a dog, etc., for all of which he

had names, was subjected to strict and diligent inquiry; and, aided by the long letters that I had received, I was able to give considerable information, on a variety of subjects.

When he and I had both become a little tired, I said, gently, "Now Grandma must go but she will come back again, very soon."

The little fellow was perfectly happy over the visit, and slept beautifully that night—dreaming, no doubt, of his dear old home and the loved ones there.

I kept up the little masquerade for about three months, and then gradually "tapered off"—finally ceasing the visits altogether: a Christmas box from home made a pretty good substitute for one visit, and he was soon becoming acquainted with his surroundings, and losing his loneliness.

I told him all about it, years afterward, when he had become a fine teacher, and one of the best grammarians that I have ever known: and he laughed over it with me, and thanked me for the bit of strategy with which we had managed to make him contented. "Otherwise. they might have had to send me back", he remarked: "and then I should probably have lost my education."

A TERRIBLE CLOUD IN THE EAST—THE DREAD
SPECTRE OF CHOLERA IN THE DISTANCE—IT
STARTS FROM INDIA—MAKES ITS WAY WEST-
WARD—REACHES NEW YORK AND OTHER
AMERICAN CITIES—VACATION SPENT AMONG
THE PATIENTS—"GOD WILL TAKE CARE OF
US, EITHER IN THIS WORLD OR THE NEXT"—
MAKING MEDICINE—HAVE THE PREMONITORY
SYMPTOMS OF THE DISEASE—STUMBLING
OVER COFFINS IN THE HALLS—END OF THE
HORRORS.

TOWARD the latter part of 1846, there
came ominous news to our Institution
—indicating that a great danger hung
above us, and was soon to fall. We
were no more alive to apprehension, in general matters, than were "seeing" people: but
it must be admitted that this news cast a
very sober feeling over our little band of students.

The dread epidemic of Cholera was coming!
There seemed no way to stop it, when it once
started on the warpath: medical methods at
that time were largely inadequate.

The disease is now better understood and
more easily fought, than in those days: Sci-

87

ence has made many long and profitable
marches since then, and brought back among
its trophies the means of stamping it out or
warding it off.

But in 1846, things were different, and it
was as good as known that the dread spectre
had started westward from the pestilence-
laden streets and jungles of India, and that it
was only a question of a little time when it
would reach American shores.

We were not long in studying up everything that could be learned on the subject:
those who read to us never had more atfen-
tive listeners than at that time. We learned
that in 1817, when the eyes of physicians were
first turned toward this disease, the frightened
inhabitants of India were calling it *"Mordechie"*
—Arabic for "Death-blow"—which suffi-
ciently indicated its terrible character. It was
said to have "originated" in a little town
named Jessore, about seventy miles northeast
of Calcutta: but that was, no doubt, merely
where the epidemic of 1846-49 was first dis-
covered.

The disease had existed for ages, in one
place and another, and even a great Roman
philosophical and medical writer named Cel-
sus, who lived in the time of the emperor Au-
gustus, made mention of it—or of something
very much like it.

So the little town of Jessore may be termed
merely the place where the terrible disease
gathered its hosts, before starting out to over-
run the world on this particular campaign.

Rapid Spread of the Cholera.

In the early part of 1846, it descended upon
Teheran, in Persia, and killed 20,000 people
before it left the place. Sometimes it would
poison one's blood all at once, and life would
be extinct in a few hours. The disease went
all over India, killed 6,380 British soldiers, as
well as unnumbered hosts of natives, and,
finally, itself an army of invasion, it drew up
its lines of attack, and advanced into Europe.

By August, 1848, it was at Berlin, and about
the close of September it reached that great
camp of "all sorts and conditions" of people—
London. Before it left England, it had taken
over 70,000 lives.

It is needless to say that all these facts were
watched with breathless anxiety, by the people
in New York. Of course there were no
cables in that day, or even any "ocean gray-
hounds": but numerous packet-ships and some
slow steamers were constantly sailing back
and forth, and news had facilities of travel, of
which it did not fail to take full advantage.

It is a problem, and, no doubt, always will
be, among physicians, and other scientists, as
to how much the matter of fear has to do with
the incurring of epidemic diseases, but one
thing is certain: New York and its kindred
American cities stood, for months, in dread of
the terrible visitation, and tremblingly expected it from day to day; and, so to speak, were
all ready to take it when it came.

As for the teachers and students in the Institution for the Blind, we of course had our
fears: but we were taught that the same good

Friend above, that had been so merciful thus far, would not desert us now; that He would do all things best for us, both in this world and the next. We rested secure in His promise that we should all be held in the hollow of His hand. And so we prayed—and waited.

We had not long to wait! On the first of December, 1848, the packet-ship "New York" landed at Staten Island. She was from Havre, and brought with her several persons who were suffering from cholera. Soon three deaths occurred in our city, and the dread disease was fighting the preliminary skirmish of its conquering march.

Everything possible in those days was done to keep the contagion down, and stamp it out; and for several months it looked as if this might be accomplished. But we were attacked from other directions.

On the 11th of December, an emigrant-ship arrived at New Orleans—having also come from Havre, leaving a few days before the "New York"; and this vessel, upon sailing into port, had already buried at sea seventeen who died of cholera. It was thought, at first, that there were no more cases on board, and the queen city of the South congratulated itself on having escaped.

But one poor sick woman, having been sent to the Charity Hospital, was soon found to be afflicted with the terrible disease; and in a few days it spread all over New Orleans—causing 3,500 deaths.

This thriving city of the South was then a

great center of travel: sailing-vessels, flat-
boats, and steamers, were constantly leaving,
in all directions. Frequently after a steam-
boat started up the river, there would be dis-
covered upon her, several cases of cholera:
and these would be hustled ashore at the first
convenient landing, and left to the care of the
hospitals, or of the people generally.

It soon reached Memphis, then St. Louis,
then Cincinnati, Chicago, etc., and on the
11th of May, 1849, New York had to ac-
knowledge that the terrible pestilence was at
last with her to stay for a time, having ob-
tained a firm foothold within her streets. Before the month was out, Albany, Philadelphia,
and Boston were all similarly afflicted; and
soon a reign of terror was at hand.

Our summer vacation began unusually
early, that year, and the students were sent to
their homes as soon as possible: but several
stayed long enough to suffer from the scourge.

Some of us remained all summer, from choice:
being convinced that God would take care of
us, and that we could be of some help. Our
faithful nurse, who had always been so kind
whenever we were ailing, refused to leave her
post; and we felt that we could afford to run
equal risks with her.

I never shall forget the terrors of that summer, in which there were, during six months,
over 5,000 deaths in New York City alone.
The harsh cry of the truckman, "Bring out
your dead!" sometimes rings in my ears to this
day.

Our Institution furnished some of these: several sickened and died almost before we could raise a hand to help them. Often the vital power seemed to ebb all at once, as soon as the victim was attacked. If we could get our patients into a state of perspiration, there was hope; and we used to rub them vigorously with salt in order to accomplish this.

Dr. J. W. Clements, who was our physician at that time, was often busy making "cholera pills"—and many a time I assisted him in their manufacture. They were of two-thirds calomel, and one-third opium—rather a "strenuous" sort of medicine for these days, it would be considered: but the necessity at that time seemed to justify the means.

One morning, I was quite sure that the dread disease had come upon me: indeed, I really had the premonitory symptoms. But I was bound that I would not yield to them: and the amount of calomel and opium that went into my stomach during those few hours. appals me as I think of it now.

All day long I kept exercising. as briskly and vigorously as I could; and when six o'clock came, I went to bed and to sleep, after having prayed to the great Physician of all, to watch over my slumber, and do with me as seemed best to Him.

In the morning, after a good night's rest, I awoke, as well as ever: and did not have any more trouble of that kind.

But the horrors of the situation grew upon us dav by day. When patients died, they were removed as quietly as possible: but I remember my fright at sometimes stumbling over coffins in the halls, on my way from room to room,

When November came, the epidemic ceased; and our school went on as usual. As above stated, several had died from among our number, and we mourned them long and deeply: but not without the reflection that they were in God's hands, and that He had His own wise purpose in taking them to Himself.

ASKED TO WRITE POEMS ON ALL SORTS OF
SUBJECTS—A DIRGE FOR DANIEL WEBSTER BE-
FORE HE WAS DEAD—DEATH OF HENRY CLAY'S
SON—POEM UPON THE SAME—THE GREAT
STATESMAN VISITS OUR INSTITUTION—HIS
PATHETIC ACTIONS AND WORDS.

ANOTHER disadvantage attendant upon
my position as a kind of poet laureate
of the Institution, was the fact that I
was expected, whenever anything un-
usual happened, to embalm the event in rhyme
and measure. I may say, too, that not only the
important events, but some of the most trivial
of subjects, have from time to time been offered
me as themes for my humble muse. People
do not always stop to reflect that a poem is
not an anecdote, or a table of statistics; and
that an incident so near and interesting to them
that they consider it worthy an epic, might be
almost ridiculous to the world at large, if set
in rhyme.

But there was and is no lack of events well
worthy any poet's best endeavor, and I
found them frequently.

I remember one evening, as I was going
through the street, with a party of friends, we

heard newsboys proclaiming the death of Daniel Webster, and offering papers for sale with full accounts of the melancholy event. "You must write a poem on the subject at once, Fanny," every one said, "while the inspiration of the sad event is on."

I went to my room, and began the mournful but (to me) interesting task. I remember commencing as follows:

"A casket has broken—a jewel has fled—
The mighty has fallen—the peerless is dead!
And the heart of the nation is bleeding once
      more,
For her eagle lies low on her desolate shore!"

I was just repeating this stanza over to my friends, so as to gather from it inspiration for the next, when a gentleman, who had come into the room in time to hear it, exclaimed, "O Fanny! Fanny! the heart of the nation isn't bleeding, or the casket broken, or the eagle lying dead on the desolate shore! That news was all a 'get-up' to sell papers: Webster *isn't* dead! Don't let the poem go on any far ther: you might kill him yet!"

I was personally glad to know that the great expounder of the Constitution "still lived"; but must say that my "muse" was a little disappointed, at having plumed herself for flight, and been ruthlessly brought down to earth again by Mr. Webster's oversight in not dying.

On the 23d of February, 1847, Henry Clay, Jr., a brave son of the magnificent statesman and orator, was killed while fighting in the

Battle of Buena Vista, in the Mexican war. I
wrote a poem on this event, and, with help of
friends, summoned courage to mail it to the
afflicted father.

The lines, which I quote from memory, were
as follows:

ON THE DEATH OF COL. CLAY.

Lo on the blood-stained battle-field,
  A wounded hero lying;
Dim is the lustre of his eye,
  For he, alas! is dying!

See, how with feeble hands he grasps
  The sword, so faithful ever!
Now drops the weapon from his side,
  To be resumed—no, never!

O gallant Clay!—though for thy brow
  Its laurels Fame is weaving,
Vain trophies these!—thy bosom now
  Its last faint sigh is heaving.

Back, tyrants!—would ye deeper make
  The wounds already given?
You, from an aged father's heart,
  Another tie have riven.

Intrepid warrior!—thou has left
  A deathless name behind thee:
That name, unsullied, bright shall shine.
  Though the dark grave may find thee!

Thou by thy General's side hast fought;
  And Taylor will deplore thee,
And many a heart that loved thee dear,
  Will weep in silence o'er thee.

Visit from Henry Clay.

It was only a short time afterward that Henry Clay visited New York, and, among other places, came to our school. He was now seventy years of age; and might easily be called one of the grandest old men of whom the country could boast. He had been in public life almost continuously for forty-three years; only three years before, he had been nominated for the Presidency, and although defeated, it was believed the Whigs would name him again for the ensuing canvass. Zachary Taylor finally received that nomination and election, and went to Washington and to death; but Clay was re-elected United States senator in the year following that, and so continued for the remainder of his life.

Of course, we were all very much flustered and "put about" at the coming of this great orator—rivalled only by Webster in his silver-tongued eloquence. We had our own band of music, containing twenty pieces; and it met him with a burst of instrumental melody.

Mr. Clay made us one of the finest addresses we had ever heard. His voice was sweet and gentle, and sympathetic in tone—qualities valued and appreciated very highly, by the blind. I remember feeling that no one of sensibility could stay in his presence very long, without being powerfully influenced by its magnetism.

He mentioned the different things he had seen on a late tour through the country—a journey that had to be made mostly by steamers and horse-coaches—vastly different from the lightning progress made by politicians nowadays, in their tours through the country. He related several pleasant incidents that occurred during the journey, and said none had been more enjoyable than the present. It was a luxury to him, he remarked, to see so many of us there, who, although the good Lord had thought fit to deprive us of our sight, were still so comfortable and so happy.

At the conclusion of this part of his speech, I heard him coming back on the platform to where I sat, and felt him take my arm. I had half hoped that he had forgotten the poem I sent him, although it was my heartfelt wish that it might give him some little comfort in his terrible affliction; but it was evidently not in his nature to forget anything kindly meant. He gently drew me toward the front of the stage, and said to the audience: "My friends, this is not the first time I have felt the comforting presence of this young friend, although I never saw her before. Into the deep wound of my sorrow, she poured the balm of consolation."

He continued to hold my arm while he talked on, in the same strain, for what seemed, to poor, shrinking me, a full hour, although it was not really more than ten minutes. I could not control my feelings, and we actually stood there and wept together.

Only five years more, and the great Kentucky orator was to rejoin the son whom he loved so fervently and lamented so deeply.

CHAPTER XX.—1848.

IN 1848, General Winfield Scott came to
see us. He was said to be a magnificent
looking man—over six feet in height,
and well proportioned; and at sixty-two,
was in the fulness of his fame; for he had, only
a few months before, entered the City of Mexico in triumph.

His career had been so splendid that we felt
as if a portion of the country's history were
about to walk in upon us.

He had commenced life at Petersburg, Va.,
which afterwards became historical in Grant's
memorable siege; he had practiced law at twenty-two, become tired of it at twenty-four, entered the army as a captain of light artillery,
and remained in it ever since. He had been
one of the heroes of 1812, and was the most

99

prominent figure of the Mexican War, which had just closed.

The General arrived a little earlier than the hour named for his reception, and I was sent down to the parlor to entertain him during the time he was waiting. I did not flatter myself that anything I might say would be of very much interest to so distinguished a man—one who had probably met many of the most illustrious statesmen and soldiers and scholars of the world; but he was quite pleasant, and insisted upon it that he was having a wonderfully good time. Of course his politeness and chivalry had much to do with his saying so, but if that was the only reason, he was a wonderfully good actor; for we fell to talking as if we had known each other a long time. Perhaps after the fatigues and anxieties of the campaign, a quiet visit with a simple girl had a restful effect upon him; but whatever the cause, he was so communicative, that I felt like asking him all sorts of questions that I would not have dared to do an hour before.

"How did it. seem, when you really found yourself in the halls of the Montezumas, General?" I asked, referring, of course, to his conquest of Mexico. "Didn't you feel like shouting?"

"No," he replied: "I felt like falling on my knees and thanking God for the victory. War is a terrible thing—demoralizing in all its immediate effects. Would to God it were not sometimes necessary, in order to accomplish results!"

He paused, and I could somehow feel that

he was thoughtfully looking into the distance with the eyes of memory—scanning once more, perhaps, "The red sand of the battlefield, with bloody corses strewn."

When, many years after this, I heard that General Sherman said, "War is hell", I thought of my conversation that day with Scott, just from his glorious victories. He was not so epigrammatic as his illustrious successor, but he meant the same thing.

At the time General Scott and I were having our conversation, Sherman was an unknown adjutant in California, only twenty-eight years old. Neither he nor the hero of Lundy's Lane perhaps had any idea that in thirteen more short years, there would be a gigantic war in this country, the like of which had never been known!

I lost my dinner by the interview (the General had had his lunch and would eat nothing), but felt well repaid, in the fact of having enjoyed a tete-a-tete with the greatest general America had thus far produced since the Revolution.

A little madcap adventure occurred after we were seated on the stage, at which I often laugh, and wonder at my own temerity. There were by this time several public men of the city, who had gathered in to see what was going on, and among them an alderman, whom I had met before, and who had the regular aldermanic love for a joke. He whispered to me, and suggested that I pull General Scott's sword from the scabbard, and hold it up over his head in regular Damocletian style. "I will guide your hand to its hilt," he said, "and you can do the rest." More like a school-girl of fourteen than a staid lady teacher in her twenties, I drew the sword suddenly from its scabbard, held it over his head, and on the impulse of the moment exclaimed, "General Scott, you are my prisoner!"

I was startled at what I had done, and apprehensive of what might follow at the alderman's odd and ill-timed joke, but was immediately relieved in mind, when the grim old warrior laughed good-naturedly, and replied, "I surrender at discretion. I always do, to the ladies. Now let me show you how to wield it." Which he did, guiding my arm with his huge soldierly hand. It was a simple incident, but one for a woman to remember as long as she lived.

After the exercises were over, he said, playfully:

"Well, Miss Fanny, I suppose that the next I hear, some one will have picked you up and run off with you."

I replied, thoughtlessly:

"Oh, no, Mr. General! *I'm* going to wait for the next President!"

I said this forgetting that he had already been talked-about as a candidate for the office; and my cheeks must have suddenly assumed a fiery red color when the fact occurred to me. But the General was safe, so far as any of us poor spinsters were concerned: he had thirty-one years before married the beautiful and accomplished Miss Mayo, of Richmond, had always been noted as a very chivalrous and devoted husband, and Mrs. Scott was still in excellent health. She was, however, not destined to grace the parlors of the White House as the first lady of the land; the General ran for President on the Whig ticket a few years later, and, much to my sorrow, was defeated.

President Polk twice gave us calls at our Institution in New York, once with his staff and we felt very much acquainted with him. He was reserved in manner, if not austere: but evidently possessed the most genial of natures. His kindly disposition was proved, through the following little incident:

Having been requested to show him some of the more interesting departments of the Institution, I was conducting him through one of the halls, when there came to our ears the voice of one of our old domestics, who had been away from us for some time, and had, evidently, just returned.

With my usual impulsiveness, I asked the President to excuse me a moment, while I ran back and greeted the dear old servant, whom I very much loved, on account of many kindnesses she had shown me at times I needed them most.

Returning to him, I made many apologies for the seeming rudeness, explained the matter as well as I could, and with burning cheeks, begged his pardon. His reply was soothing and reassuring, and convinced me that under his quiet exterior, was a sympathetic and generous nature. "I am glad you went back, little girl," he said: "it shows that you have a kind heart, and a due appreciation of real worth."

Of course everything was read up and talked up in our school, concerning the different people of distinction who visited us: and President Polk's ancestry was ventilated from "way back." When we found that the original family in Ireland was named "Pollock", we immediately wondered whether he was not some relation to Robert Pollok, author of "The Course of Time"—which we had heard read with great interest. Our genealogical enthusiasm was, ere long, somewhat dampened by one of the teachers' discovering that the distinguished Robert was a Scotchman, and spelled his name without a "c." I have since learned, however, that there are Scotch-Irishmen and Irish-Scotchmen; and that names are occasionally modified in other countries, as well as our own, on their way through the generations.

NAPOLEON'S FAITHFUL MARSHAL, BERTRAND—
A POEM OF WELCOME—HOW HE WATCHED
BONAPARTE'S LIFE EBB AWAY—LAURA BRIDG-
MAN, AND HER SWEETNESS OF MAGNETISM—
JENNY LIND COMES AND SINGS TO THE BLIND
STUDENTS—HER GENEROSITY—THE GREAT
AND ONLY BARNUM—ALICE CARY—A POEM
FROM FRANCES RIDLEY HAVERGAL.

GENERAL HENRI GRATIEN BER-
TRAND, on his trip to this country,
made a visit to our Institution at
about this time. We were all very much
interested in him, because he was one of the
few surviving men who knew and were near
the person of Napoleon Bonaparte, during a
large portion of his career.

Bertrand was one of the bravest and most
faithful of the "Little Corporal's" aids, and in
any ordinary war or series of wars, would have
shone forth preeminent. But it took more-
than-giants to do that in the vast Napoleonic
conflicts, and Bertrand never ranked among
the Neys, the Murats, and the McDonalds.

We remembered, however, the fact that he
had worked his way up from a captaincy of en-
gineers, had been an efficient and constantly

growing soldier through the Italian-Egyptian campaigns, and had participated in the beams of glory that came flashing upon the French at Austerlitz. We knew that after the disastrous battle of Aspern, he restored the passage across the Danube for the French troops, and did much toward saving the Emperor's army; and that for this service he was made count, and governor of Illyria. We had heard that at the battle of Waterloo he helped restrain Napoleon from rushing into certain death; and that when his chief was exiled to St. Helena, he went with him, stayed there till he saw him die, and afterwards helped bring his body back to Paris, when, as Victor Hugo said, "an exiled coffin returned in triumph" He now lies near Napoleon in the gorgeous tomb at the Hôtel des Invalides, Paris, under the famous gilded dome: many of my readers have no doubt seen his name there.

When Bertrand came to see us, I was as usual deputed to write a poem of welcome; and had the honor of reading it before him. In it I depicted him as sitting pensively with his head bowed upon his hands, seeing Napoleon's life ebb away.

"How did you know that?" he asked me, referring to those lines, during our short conversation. "How did you know that I was in that position?"

"I did *not* 'know' it", I replied: "I merely imagined it."

"It was just the way I *did* sit, through all that fearful night, until I saw Napoleon's eyes close, and knew that he was gone", replied Bertrand.

He seemed somehow to have detected in the poem a little higher praise of himself than of his royal master; and perhaps felt more resentment than gratitude at the fact. He asked me if I were not an admirer of Napoleon. "I admired him *as a soldier*", I replied, and stopped, only telling half the truth. He did not press the question any farther, and the interview soon came to an end.

Indeed, while I recognized the bravery and faithfulness of General Bertrand, I could not help wishing all the time that his efforts had been put forth in the service of some better chief; and it may be that fragments of that thought became mingled with the poem.

From the contemplation of war and warriors, the step to dear sweet Laura Bridgman is a long one, but most grateful. I well remember the first time I met her. It was in Washington: and I had heard so much about her and her wonderful achievements, that she seemed to me fully as much of a curiosity as anybody in the great national capital. I knew that at the age of two years she had lost her sight, her hearing, and her speech; and that the senses of touch and smell were also considerably impaired. She was given her first instruction at the age of eight, by the well-known Dr. Howe. He could communicate with her only by the touch of the fingers; and his first effort was to make her understand the analogy between objects and the words representing them. She finally commenced to understand what was wanted, and to recognize the words, produced in raised letters. Then the letters were dis-arranged; she was taught to put them back in their proper places, and in this way learned to spell.

It took her some time to realize that here was a means through which she could commu-nicate with her fellow-beings, but when she did, her happiness is said to have been pa-thetic. After this she soon learned the manual alphabet, and by degrees acquired as much miscellaneous knowledge as most people whom she met. She took lessons on the piano, and became a skilful performer; could do fine needle-work, and attend efficiently to many household duties.

A girl who, though deaf, dumb, and blind, could do all these things (and many others, of more importance) was certainly a wonder: and in whatever circle she moved, Laura Bridg-man was "the observed of all observers."

She was fully aware of these facts, for every-thing said about her was faithfully reported by her comrades in the party, through the means of their nimble and talkative fingers; but she continued as modest and sensible as ever, and did not show the least undue pride in her suc-cess as a public character. She soon became very intimate with many of her New York friends, and one of my sweetest recollections is of her, sitting upon my lap, twining her arms around my neck, and then spelling out for me the name, "Little Fan"—to distinguish me

from another one of our band, who bore the
same given name as myself, and was larger in
size.

But words, with us, were hardly needed : we
could almost understand each other's thoughts
by the magnetism that flashed between us. I
do not remember a sweeter personality than
Laura Bridgman's.

When Jenny Lind came to this country, in
1850, one of the first places she visited, was our
Institution ; and a very pleasant memory is the
beautiful music and the cordial hand-shakings
she gave us. She had already conquered Europe with the melody of her voice and the goodness of her heart ; and all America was wild
to hear her. The first concert at which she
appeared in New York netted her $10,000 ; and
she immediately donated the entire sum to
charity.

This, of course, made her much more popular than ever ; for there are few things that
people like better, than to get value received
for their money, and then have it paid back to
them.

We tried hard to induce the gentle cantatrice
to make us a speech ; but this she declined to
attempt, although having a very good command of English. She sang for us, however,
again and again. And such singing !

Of course, during this particular time,
wherever Jenny Lind went, the great and in-
evitable Barnum followed not far behind. I
knew him exceedingly well, and can say that
with all his shrewdness, he had many kind and

generous traits of character. This conundrum used to be printed and reprinted in the newspapers of that date:

"Why are Jenny Lind and Barnum well calculated always to agree, and never have any difficulty?—Because one is always for giving, and the other is always for getting!"

But Barnum made many munificent donations—which were of no less benefit to the world, though partly advertisements.

Among the sweet memories of the past, is that of Alice Cary, with whom I corresponded for a time, and from whom I had many a pleasant word of cheer. I used also to have letters from Frances Ridley Havergal; and well remember how delighted I was, once, at receiving a poem from her, dedicated to me, which read as follows:

AN ENGLISH TRIBUTE TO FANNY CROSBY.

Sweet blind singer over the sea,
Tuneful and jubilant, how can it be
That the songs of gladness, which float so far,
As if they fell from the evening star,
Are the notes of one who never may see
"Visible music" of flower and tree,
Purple of mountain, or glitter of snow,
Ruby and gold of the sunset glow,
And never the light of a loving face?
Must not the world be a desolate place
For eyes that are sealed with the seal of years,
Eyes that are open only for tears?
How can she sing in the dark like this?
What is her fountain of light and bliss?

Poem from *Frances Ridley Havergal.*

Oh, her heart can see, her heart can see!
And its sight is strong and swift and free;
Never the ken of mortal eye
Could pierce so deep and far and high
As the eagle-vision of hearts that dwell
In the lofty, sunlit citadel
Of faith that overcomes the world,
With banners of hope and joy unfurled,
Garrisoned with God's perfect peace,
Ringing with pæans that never cease,
Flooded with splendor bright and broad—
The glorious light of the love of God!

Her heart can see, her heart can see!
Well may she sing so joyously!
For the King Himself, in His tender grace,
Hath shown her the brightness of His face;
And who shall pine for a glow-worm light
When the sun goes forth in his radiant might?
She can read His law as a shining chart,
For His finger hath written it on her heart;
She can read His love, for on all her way
His hand is writing it every day.
"Bright cloud", indeed, must that darkness be,
Where "Jesus only" the heart can see!

Her heart can see, her heart can see,
Beyond the glooms and the mystery,
Glimpses of glory not far away,
Nearing and brightening day by day ·
Golden crystal and emerald bow,
Lustre of pearl and sapphire glow,
Sparkling river and healing tree,
Evergreen palms of victory,

Harp and crown and raiment white,
Holy and beautiful dwellers in light;
A throne, and One thereon, whose face
Is the glory of that glorious place!

Dear blind sister over the sea,
An English heart goes forth to thee!
We are linked by a cable of faith and song,
Flashing bright sympathy swift along;
One in the east and one in the west,
Singing for Him whom our souls love best;
"Singing for Jesus", telling His love,
All the way to our home above,
Where the severing sea, with its restless tide,
Never shall hinder, and never divide.
Sister, what will our meeting be,
When our hearts shall sing and our eyes shall
see!

STARTING FOR A LECTURE.

CHAPTER XXII.—1850-1868.

D URING the fifties and sixties, I wrote the words of several songs, which became popular, and continued so for many years.

One of these was "Rosalie, the Prairie Flower"; another was "Glad to Get Home"; another "Proud World, Good-bye"; and still another, "There's Music in the Air." These were set to notes by George F. Root, and sold in thousands of copies in sheet music and other forms, throughout the country.

Several cantatas also constituted part of my pen-work during this time. Among these were "The Flower Queen" and "The Pilgrim Fathers"—the music of the latter having been composed jointly by George F. Root and Lowell Mason.

But in 1864 commenced the real and most important work of my life, so far as poetry was concerned. In that year, the late Peter Stryker, one of the most excellent of men, in-

113

troduced me to William B. Bradbury, who was already famous as a writer of hymn-music.

Mr. Bradbury received me with a cordiality that made me feel immediately that we could work together: poet and composer cannot always do that "For many years, I have been wanting you to write for me," he said, "but somehow could not get opportunity to talk with you on the subject. I wish you would begin, right away."

It now seemed to me as if the great work of my life had really begun: and I commenced the delicious toil which, with an occasional pause for rest, I have continued ever since.

If at any time I have been tempted to leave this work, and turn my poetical efforts in other directions, I have invariably been brought back and spurred to fresh vigor, by the memory of a dream that I had, not long before my taking of this, what seemed to me a sacred, trust.

It was really more than a dream—more even than a vision: it was a kind of reality—with my senses all at their fullest, though the body was asleep.

I was in an immense observatory, and before me the largest telescope I had ever imagined. I could see everything plainly (for, in my most vivid dreams, the sense of sight appears fully restored). Looking in the direction pointed out by my friend, I saw a very bright and captivating star, and was gradually carried toward it—past other stars, and any amount of celestial scenery that I have not strength even to describe.

At last we came to a river, and paused there. "May I not go on?" I asked of my guide. "Not now, Fanny", was the reply. "You must return to the earth and do your work there, before you enter those sacred bounds; but ere you go, I will have the gates opened a little way, so you can hear one burst of the eternal music."

Soon there came chords of melody such as I never had supposed could exist anywhere: the very recollection of it thrills me. And in the writing of my hymns, the memory of that journey toward the star, always cheers and inspires me.

The first one I wrote for Mr. Bradbury, was the hymn that begins:

> "We are going, we are going,
>   To a home beyond the skies,
> Where the roses never wither,
>   And the sunlight never dies."

Others followed, in rapid succession; and for four years, almost until the date of my associate's death, we continued to work together in that capacity. Three volumes of hymns—each containing from thirty to forty of mine —were published by Mr. Bradbury. Of all these, perhaps the one having the widest circulation, was that which contained the hymn beginning:

> "There's a cry from Macedonia."

As I often composed as many as six or seven hymns in one day, there were more of them in the aggregate than Mr. Bradbury could set to music; and the late Philip Phillips, a most genial and lovable man, took several of them for his own compositions.

From this large number of hymns that I composed, selections were made: some were put aside and never used. I made no pretense of being able to do this selecting myself—it was always performed by others; and I often find myself wondering whether some hymn may not have been suppressed, that was of real merit, while others less worthy, were put to the fore. One cannot always determine at first sight, concerning products of the pen, which will most forcibly strike the public mind and heart.

But Mr. Bradbury was not strong, physically; and in 1868 he died. "I know I am not going to live very long," he used to say: "but, Fanny, you must take up the work where I leave it."

At his funeral, in Montclair, N. J., the first hymn sung was that with which we had commenced our work together—

> "We are going, we are going,
> To a home beyond the skies."

It is needless to say that the exercises affected me more deeply than almost anything I had ever experienced. As I stood for a minute by the casket which held the honored dead, I could not refrain from sobs and tears; but all at once I heard a clear beautiful voice from the congregation, saying:

"Fanny, pick up the work where Mr. Bradbury leaves it; take your harp from the willow, and dry your tears."

I could never learn who spoke these words, although there were several others who distinctly heard them; but they came to my ears very plainly, and I can hear them now.

"We see so many of your hymns in our books!" often say new friends to me: "How many you must have written!" But they are often not aware that hundreds more—not with my name attached, but bearing different nomde-plumes, are from my pen. I cannot now even remember all the different names, over a hundred in number, I have used; but among them are "Mrs. E. A. Andrew", "Ella Dale", "Julia Stirling", "Victoria Francis", "Victoria Stewart", "Lyman Cuyler", "Charles Bruce", "Lizzie Edwards", "Grace I. Francis", "Sally M. Smith", "Henrietta Blain", "Myra Judson", "Charles Burns", "Alice Monteith", "James M. Black", "Frank Gould", "Jennie Garnett", "Victoria Stirling", "Carrie M. Wilson", "Maud Marion", etc., etc.

Among many other incidents connected with my hymns, is one related to me by Mr. Ira B. Sankey, who has long been, and is still, one of my dearest friends. When he was in Edinburgh, an old Scotch woman came to him, and said she wanted to thank him for writing "Safe in the Arms of Jesus." "But I didn't write it," replied Mr. Sankey: "that was Fanny Crosby";—and he sat down and told her about me.

"Weel," said the old lady, when he was through, "when ye gang back to America, gie hei my love, an' tell her an auld Scots woman sends her blessing. The last hymn my daughter sang before she died, was that one."

There are many other hymns that have been widely used, and concerning which I could relate many (to me) interesting reminiscences. Among these are "Rescue the Perishing", "Speed Away", "Pass Me Not", "I Am Thine", etc., etc.

I am sometimes asked how many hymns I have written in my lifetime. This question I am unable to answer accurately; but am safe in saying that the number reaches over five thousand.

I may be able, some time, to remember the names of all those who have done my hymns the honor of setting them to music, but have not the leisure just at present. If there should be subsequent editions of this book, I can perhaps include them. Besides those already mentioned and to be mentioned, stand out prominently Prof. H. R. Palmer and Mr. Hubert P. Main—both of whom are among my friends still living.

CHAPTER XXIII.—1853-1893.

I N 1853, our head teacher, Prof. William Cleveland, was called to New Jersey by the death of his father, a Presbyterian clergyman. After a few days' absence, he returned, bringing with him his brother, a youth of sixteen; and the next morning afterward he came to consult me in regard to "the boy."

"Grover has taken our father's death very much to heart," he said, "and I wish you would go into the office, where I have installed him as clerk, and talk with him, once in a while."

So I went down as requested, and was introduced to the young man—not dreaming, of course, that I was conversing with one destined to be twice elected to the chief magistracy of our nation.

We talked together unreservedly about **his** father's death, and a bond of friendship sprung up between us, which was strengthened by subsequent interviews. He seemed a very gentle, but intensely ambitious boy, and I felt that there were great things in store for him—although, as above intimated, there was no thought in my mind that he would ever be chosen from among the millions of this country, to be its President.

Whether the death of his father had settled his mind into a serious view, or whether it was because industry and perseverance were natural to him, 1 do no' know: but think each of these influences bore a part toward directing his actions.

He very seldom went out to a party or entertainment with others of the same age: but remained in his room, working away at his books. I am told that during his entire career, this faculty of hard and almost incessant work, has been one of his most valuable aids.

Among other very pleasant characteristics which I noticed in him, was a disposition to help others, whenever possible. Knowing that it was a great favor to me to have my poems copied neatly and legibly, he offered to perform that service for me: and I several times availed myself of his aid.

One day, just as he had finished transcribing from my memory a poem somewhat longer than usual, the man who was superintendent at that time came suddenly into the office. This was not the same gentleman who had greeted me so kindly upon my arrival, **and** given me such good advice: but a successor, who, although wishing no doubt to do **his** duty, was unable at times to control his temper.

Seeing at a glance what young Mr. Grover Cleveland had been doing for me, he remonstrated, violently: gave me to understand that the clerks in the office had other work to do, than to copy my poetry; and hurried out of the room.

The whole affair occurred in such a whirl-wind of bad humor, that I was dumbfounded, and did not know what to say or how to act. I was conscious of having done no harm in allowing the young man to write down my poetry for me, and knew not whether to rave, or to adopt the good old feminine remedy of indulging in a few straightforward tears.

To my great surprise, young Mr. Cleveland broke into a low but very decided laugh. "We are entirely within our rights, Fanny," he explained, "and he had no business to interrupt or reproach us. Tomorrow, at this time, come down here with another poem; I will copy it for you; he will step into the office again, as he generally does at this time; he will no doubt 'start in' to administer to you another 'going over'; and then, if I were you, I would give him a few paragraphs of plain prose, that he would not very soon forget."

The whole event turned as Grover had foretold. The superintendent came in, just as the young man was finishing up another poem; and commenced a second series of reproaches.

But I had my "prose" all ready : and imparted it to the gentleman at once. I reminded him, in as mild a voice as I could, but as firm a one as was necessary, under the circumstances, that I was a teacher there, and had rights, as well as he; that my poems had been used largely for the benefit of the Institution, and that the reciting of them had not been without its mission in calling new students to us; that under such circumstances, I should claim the help of the attachés of the school, whenever they were willing to give it, without neglecting other duties; and that if he ever referred to the subject again, I should ask the trustees what *they* thought about it.

"You will never have any more trouble with him", laughed young Mr. Cleveland, the next time we met.

This prediction proved true: the same sagacity that has since been used in the manipulation of cabinets and councils, had, almost in its very beginnings, come to the aid of a poor blind teacher.

I have since had the privilege of a very pleasant acquaintance with my boy-amanuensis: I have traced him through the different offices in which he has been entrusted with the public interests of his fellow-countrymen; have been at his home, been greeted by his sweet and accomplished wife, and held his children in my arms; and have always found him, in spirit, the same modest, sensible boy, that copied my poems years ago.

CHAPTER XXIV.—1893-1903.

THE MAKING OF A HYMN—THE "HYMN-WORK-
SHOP"—"MOODS" IN WRITING—"BUILDING" A
MOOD—BEGINNING WITH PRAYER—MEASURE
AND TUNE—WRITING TO AN AIR—THE BOOKS
OF THE MIND—HYMNS WAITING FOR THEIR
MATES.

TRUE hymns may be said, in one sense, to make themselves; although they must be given human instruments through which to work. No one should ever attempt to write a hymn, unless the ideas flow easily and naturally. But how is this to be brought about?—Some details of personal experience may not be uninteresting to the readers of this book—nearly all of whom are likely to be more or less interested in the subject.

"Take us into the hymn-workshop or laboratory", friends sometimes say to me. "Let us know your processes of thought, of feeling, of accomplishment. Give us the steps you employ, as nearly as possible, in constructing a hymn."

Well, I will, as accurately as I can. Maybe this chapter will inspire others to write sacred songs that shall do good in the future.

There is a great deal said nowadays, and I

123

do not know but there always has been, about "moods" in writing. There is much truth in the doctrine. There are some days, or at least hours, when I could not compose a hymn if the world were laid at my feet as a promised recompense. Fancy writing verses when one has that "hell of a' diseases", as Robbie Burns called it, the toothache! The silent cry of the suffering molar would run through it all. Imagine yourself trying to get into sweet accord with Heaven while your nerves were suffering from neuralgia! It could not be done. Sick people have written good poetry, but I fancy it was in their intervals of partial convalescence.

I am not subject to very many unpleasant sensations on account of ill health: the good Lord has given me a sound constitution, and a body which, though not particularly strong in appearance, is fitted to endure. But there are times when I am not in the mood to write, and when, as I said above, it would not be possible for me immediately to compose a hymn.

So what would I do, if it were necessary or highly desirable that a hymn be written on a certain day or night: as, for some occasion, or some work soon to be published?—If I were not in the mood to write, I would build a mood—or, try to draw one around me.

l should sit alone, as I have done on many a day and night, praying God to give me the thoughts and the feelings wherewith to compose my hymn. After a time—perhaps not unmingled with struggle—the ideas would come, and I would soon be happy in my verse.

It may seem a little old-fashioned, always to begin one's work with prayer: but I never undertake a hymn without first asking the good Lord to be my inspiration in the work that I am about to do.

Although, of course, I cannot read a printed book, having been deprived of sight almost from birth, yet, while composing, I feel happier and more at ease, if I hold a small volume in my hand. This may be a matter of habit: during my many years of teaching, I always kept a small book in my hands; and in reciting my own poems to audiences, I follow the same method.

When at last I have arrived at the proper stage of thought and feeling, and am sure that I am in condition to reach the minds and hearts of my constituency, and sing to them something worthy for them to hear, I cast about, for a few minutes, as to the measure, and, possibly, the tune.

Much more depends upon this, than might at first seem to be the case. For if there is a false accent or a mistake in the metre, the hymn cannot stand much chance of proving a success; or at least its possibilities are very much lessened. Among the millions of hymns that have been sung and forgotten, many contain no doubt deep and pious thought and feeling, but have been crippled and killed by the roughness of some line, or the irregularity of one or more measures.

Often I take in my mind some tune already

well known, as a model, or, perhaps, more accurately speaking, as a guide, and work to it.
This, however, does not imply that the tune
will ultimately be chosen as the companion of
the words: for it has probably already its own
true and lawful mate, with which it is to be
happy and useful. Sometimes a tune is furnished me for which to write the words.

"Blesséd Assurance" was made in this manner. My dear friend, Mrs. Joseph F. Knapp,
so well known as a writer and singer of most
exquisite music, and as an aid and inspiration
to all who know her, had composed the tune,
and it seemed to me one of the sweetest I
had heard for a long time. She asked me to
write a hymn for it, and I felt, while bringing
the words and tones together, that the air and
the hymn were intended for each other. In
the many hundred times that I have heard it
sung, this opinion has been more and more
confirmed.

After any particular hymn is done, I let it lie
for a few days in the writing-desk of my mind,
so to speak, until I have leisure to prune it, to
read it through with the eyes of my memory,
and in other ways mould it into as presentable
shape as possible. I often cut, trim, and
change it.

"How can you remember a hymn?" I am
often asked. To this I need only reply that
recollecting is not entirely a lost art, although
we live in rushing days of memorandum-
tablets and carefully kept journals and ledgers.
The books of the mind are just as real and tan-

gible as those of the desk and the library-shelves—if we only will use them enough to keep their binding flexible, and their pages free from dust.

I have no trouble in sorting and arranging my literary and lyric wares within the apartments of my mind. If I were given a little while in which to do it, I could take down from its shelves, hundreds if not thousands of hymns, that I have written during the sixty years in which I have been praising my Redeemer through this medium of song. Do not let go to decay and ruin those vast interior regions of thought and feeling, good brother or sister! Your memory would be much to you if you were ever deprived of some of the organs of sense that now so distract you from deep and continued thought.

After the hymn is finished, and transcribed by some friend, it generally waits for its tune, and steadfastly hopes that it will succeed in making a matrimonial alliance, and a good one. I have had the advantage, for the most part, of very sympathetic and talented composers.

After Mr. Bradbury's death, I wrote many hymns for W. H. Doane, who composed much beautiful music. One day he came to me hurriedly, and exclaimed: "Fanny, I have just forty minutes to catch the cars for Cincinnati; during that time you must write me a hymn, and give me a few minutes to catch the train."

I happened to be in a good mood for writing: he hummed the melody to which he wanted the words written; and in fifteen minutes I gave them to him, and he started away. Upon his arrival home, he published them; and I have been told upon good authority that the hymn is now sung wherever Christian music is known. Many of the readers of this book no doubt, are familiar with it. It begins as follows:

"Safe in the arms of Jesus,
  Safe on his gentle breast,
There by his love o'ershadowed,
  Sweetly my soul shall rest."

The writing of the hymn, "All the Way My Saviour Leads Me", was the result of a bit of personal experience. One day, I wanted the modestly substantial amount of five dollars for a particular purpose, and needed it very badly. I did not know, just then, exactly how to get it: and was led in my mind to pray for it. Somehow, I knew the good Lord would give it to me if I asked him for it—though exactly how, I did not know.

Not long after I had prayed for the money, a gentleman came into the house, "passed the time of day", shook hands with me, and went out immediately. When I closed my hand, after the friendly salutation, I found in it a five-dollar bill, which he had left there.

I have no way to account for this, except to believe that God, in answer to my prayer, put it into the heart of this good man, to bring me the money.

My first thought, after finding out the pe-

BEFORE AN AUDIENCE.

cuniary value of this little silken reminder of friendship and regard, was,

"In what a wonderful way the Lord helps me! All the way my Saviour leads me!"

I immediately wrote the hymn, and Dr. Robert Lowry, the famous clergyman-hymn-writer, set it to music.

I could mention here, many and many a case, in which I have had direct answer to prayer. I have never had the least reason to doubt the practical usefulness of that promise that if we ask we shall receive. Our Saviour is so willing not only to lead us, but to supply our wants, if we will only ask him!

CHAPTER XXV.—1900.

A POEM BY WILL CARLETON.

WHILE I was visiting at the home of my constant and loving friends, Mr. and Mrs. Will Carleton, in Brooklyn, New York, on my eightieth birthday Mr. Carleton wrote the following poem, which I insert here, not from vanity, I am sure my readers will believe, but with a desire to place on record my happiness at some of the kind things that have been said about me.

Song-bird in the dark,
Adding each day unto our lyric treasure,
    And rising, like the lark,
Nearer to heaven for each ecstatic measure:

    Sing on, O rich, clear voice,
'Mid the world's clamor for the world's possession;
    Thou art the angels' choice
To give their sweetest anthems earth-expression!

    Love on, O gentle heart,
To all mankind with stately pureness clinging;

130

Poem by Will Carleton.

The followers of thy art,
With lips devout caress thee in their singing!

In myriad temples grand,
Through whose broad aisles the organ-tones
    are pealing,
Thy words walk hand in hand
With truths the rich-bound Bible is revealing.

By many a cottage door,
Where .Faith and Love with Poverty are dwell-
    ing,
Thy sweet words, o'er and o'er,
The mother to her new-found babe is telling.

Where arctic snow-storms sweep,
Where tropic ghosts a hand to death are reach-
    ing,
Thy jeweled words still keep
Their tryst with God, and aid His solemn
    teaching.

Song-bird in the light,
Thou shalt see splendors when this world's
    have faded!
E'en now thy path is bright
With stars in heaven, whose kindling thou hast
    aided.

Yearn on, O lofty soul,
Though voices from the song-land intercede
    thee!
Spurn not this earth's control
Yet many years: our suffering mortals need
    thee.

But when at last The King
Shall bid thy friends above to cease their wait-
    ing,
  The angel-choirs will sing,
To welcome thee, some hymn of thy creating.

  And Christ will be thy guide,
Confirming, step by step, His wondrous story;
  And seek the Father's side,
And say, "She taught the world to sing Thy
    glory."

CHAPTER XXVI.—1843-1903.

OLDEST AND NEWEST HYMNS.

I AM often asked, "Do you write as many hymns as ever?" Perhaps not, quite: but this is owing to the fact that I spend so much time visiting churches in different parts of the country, and speaking, and reading my poems to audiences.

My relations with Christian Endeavor Societies, and Young Men's Christian Associations, are also very intimate and friendly: and I often address them. I wear a gold badge of membership, presented me by one of the Railroad Branches of the Y. M. C. A.

I include in this chapter some of my earliest and some of my latest hymns: others can be found in various hymn-books. In one of those here published, it will be noticed. words and music are both by myself: but I have heretofore been content to write the words. and let others furnish the music. This is the only case in which I have departed from the rule.

While writing my earlier poems, I did not attempt hymns: although my mind was often drawn in that direction. I greatly admired the grand productions of Watts, Wesley, Montgomery, and others: but it did not then occur to me that I could write hymns that people would care to sing.

Everything in this world is progressive, and courage and ambition are no exception to the rule. I seem to have been led, little by little, toward my life-work.

Often, in those early days, would come over me the inclination to write hymns: but I resisted it, or, what amounted to about the same thing, let it go by default.

Still, as the sweetness and grandeur of the religion of our Saviour sank into my heart, I felt more and more like putting my feelings into rhythm. And, if my friends will pardon me for perhaps giving the matter too much importance, I will say, that the following stanzas, one of the few distinctly religious poems of my first book, constituted my first hymn:

EVENING HYMN.

Ps. IV:8—"I will both lay me down in peace and sleep; for thou, Lord, only, makest me to dwell in safety."

Drawn is the curtain of the night,
  Oh 'tis the sacred hour of rest;
Sweet hour, I hail thee with delight,
  Thrice welcome to my weary breast.

O God to thee my fervent prayer,
  I offer, kneeling at thy feet;
Tho' humbly breathed, O deign to hear—
  Smile on me from the mercy seat!

While angels round their watches keep,

Whose harps thy praise unceasing swell,
"I lay me down in peace and sleep",
  For thou in safety mak'st me dwell.

Drawn is the curtain of the night,
  Thou bid'st creation silent be,
And now, with holy calm delight,
  Father, I would commune with thee.

Shepherd of Israel, deign to keep
  And guard my soul from every ill;
Thus will I lay me down, and sleep,
  For thou in safety mak'st me dwell.

The following is, so far as I can remember
my second hymn:

EASTER SUNDAY.

Hail, sacred morn! When from the tomb
  The son of God arose;
"Captivity he captive led",
  And triumphed o'er his foes.

Rejoice! O holy church, rejoice!
  Awake thy noblest strain!
Put off thy weeds of mourning, now,
  The Saviour lives again.

Oh let thy loud hosannas reach
  The portals of the sky,
Where angels tune their gentle harps,
  And heavn'ly choirs reply.

Glory to God—He ever lives
  To plead our cause above;
He—He is worthy to receive
  All honor, power, and love.

Hail, mighty King!—we at thy feet
  Our grateful homage pay;
Accept the humble sacrifice
  And wash our sins away.

Then, at the resurrection morn,
  When the last trump shall sound,
May we awake to life anew,
  And with thy saints be found.

Another attempt at distinctively sacred
poetry, made about this same time, and which
may be considered my third hymn, was as
follows:

CHRISTMAS HYMN.

How tranquil, how serene the night,
  When to the sleepy earth,
A heavenly host of seraphs bright,
  Proclaimed a Saviour's birth!

The shepherds on Judea's plains,
  With wonder heard their songs:
"Glory to God! to Him alone,
  Our highest praise belongs!

"Glory to God!"—through Heaven's broad
    arch,
  The sacred chorus ran:
"Good will, and never-ending peace,
  Henceforth to mortal man.

"Glory to God! let all the earth,
  To Him their honors bring,
And every heart, and every tongue,
  His praise responsive sing!"

Only Hymn Set to Music by Self.

The following are from some of my newest hymns, and, in relation to those given, represent an interval of perhaps sixty years—during which time I have almost constantly been busy writing hymns of varying merit:

SPRING HYMN.

Words and Music by Fanny Crosby.

1. The winds have ceased their moaning, The win-ter storms have passed;
2. The world is full of sun-shine, The birds are on the wing.

The love-ly face of Na-ture Is wreathed in smiles at last.
From dis-tant climes they hast-en To greet the gen-tle spring.

The pearl-y streams no lon-ger In i-cy chains are bound;
There's mu-sic in the for-est, A-mid the branch-es fair;

The mountains glow with ver-dure, The hills with joy re-sound.
There's mu-sic in the val-ley, And beau-ty ev-ery where.

O thou whose love beholdeth
  The world thy hand hath mane.
Creator, Lord, Redeemer,
  In majesty arrayed!
We praise thee for the spring time,
  And all its golden hours,
For lake and sparkling fountain,
  For sunshine, birds, and flowers.

And when thy voice shall call us
  To yonder blissful shore,
Where spring abideth ever
  And winter comes no more,
Beside the crystal river,
  Among the ransomed throng,
We'll blend our harps triumphant
  In one eternal song.

137

While at a meeting of the "Farther Lights", at the residence of Mrs. Will Carleton, the Founder of the Society, I was elected a member, and a badge of the Order was pinned upon me. This, I was proud to know, took place in the very parlor where occurred the first meeting of Farther Lights ever held.

I was inspired to write a hymn for these loved sisters in the missionary-cause; and soon sent them the following:

SPEED ON, O LIGHT!

Speed on thy glorious mission,
    O light of purest love,
Whose radiant beams were kindled
    In Edenland above;
Speed on where those that languish
    In sorrow's dreary nights,
Shall feel the joy thou bringest,
    And hail the Farther Lights!

O band of Christian workers,
    With whom I oft have met,
Whose voices kind and gentle
    I hear in memory yet—
In this my prayer ascending
    My inmost soul unites—
God bless the Christian circle
    We call the Farther Lights!

God bless your heartfelt labor,
    My youthful sisters dear,

The World for Christ.

And grant you strength and courage
  Through grace to persevere;
Till India's happy greeting
  With Afric's song unites;
While on the flaming watch-tower
  Still shine the Farther Lights!

THE WORLD FOR CHRIST—A NEW-YEAR RALLY-
ING SONG.

Air, "From Greenland's Icy Mountains."

Arise, O Christian soldiers,
  And consecrate anew
Your all upon the altar,
  Of Him who died for you!
Arise in faith united,
  And let this year record
Your undivided service,
  To Christ, our risen Lord!

Oh, rally 'round His standard;
  Defend the cross you love;
And look to Him for wisdom
  And counsel from above.
Against the arch deceiver,
  Against the host of sin,
March on with steady purpose
  The world for Christ to win!

Be strong, O Christian soldiers,
  On Jesus cast your care!

And when the conflict rages
  Let ev'ry breath be prayer.
Fear not; the Lord is with you:
  'Tis He who speaks within;
March on with zeal and courage
  The world for Christ to win!

Go forth, go forth rejoicing,
  And in the Master's name,
To weary souls that perish,
  Eternal life proclaim!
The crowning day is coming;
  The end of toil and sin;
March on through grace determined
  The world for Christ to win!

CHRIST HATH RISEN.

Airs, "St. George"; "Mary to the Saviour's Tomb."

Still and silent as the night,
Holy angels robed in light
Came and rolled the stone away,
From the tomb where Jesus lay.
Backward, trembling, pale with dread,
Lo, the arch-deceiver fled,
When the Prince of Life arose,
Mighty Conqueror o'er His foes!

Strike your harps, ye saints on high!
With your anthems fill the sky!

Hymn to Summer.

Ye who sang "a Saviour born",
Hail His resurrection morn!
Jesus lives the world to save:
Where thy triumph, boasting grave?
Death is vanquished, bound in chains;
Christ, our Lord, forever reigns!

On this bright and glorious day,
When the faithful meet to pray,
Bring the Easter lilies fair,
Nature's gems of beauty rare.
Let the organ's lofty strain
Thrill our raptured souls again;
Christ hath risen from the tomb,
Clothed in Heav'n's immortal bloom!

HYMN TO SUMMER.

O summer, lovely summer,
  We hail thy golden hours,
And welcome back the sunshine
  That wakes thy dewy flowers;
The queenly rose and lily
  Adorn each rural spot,
And greet their gentle sister,
  The sweet forget-me-not.

The fields are white with daisies,
  The hills are green and fair;
The merry birds are singing—
  There's music everywhere.
The brook and sparkling fountain
  Have caught the tuneful strain,

While echoes from the forest
　　Ring out their glad refrain.

O summer, lovely summer,
　　In all thy bright array,
New hopes and joys unfolding
　　With each returning day!
The promised tune of harvest
　　Thy coming soon will bring;
And o'er the sheaves he gathers,
　　The reaper's heart will sing!

HARVEST HYMN.

Air, "I Shall See the King in His Beauty."

All hail to the days that are coming,
　　How lovely the blue ether sky;
The fields in their beauty are smiling,
　　The harvest already is nigh.
The voice of the brook and the fountain,
　　The song of the bird and the bee,
Their carol in harmony blending,
　　Are happy as happy can be.

Lo, yonder the queen of the harvest
　　Comes forth as the toilers appear,
And waving her chaplet of lilies
　　She greets them with mirth and good cheer.
Now thrust in your sickles, ye reapers,
　　And gather the ripe golden grain;
The Lord has rewarded your labor,
　　And crowned it with plenty again.

Ode to Thanksgiving.

The seed that you scattered in springtime
  Grew up with the fruits and the flowers,
Refreshed with the joy-laden zephyrs
  The sunshine, the dew, and the showers.
And oh, when the sheaves you have garnered,
  Be mindful His love to recall,
And praise with your highest devotion
  The bountiful giver of all!

O land, by the God of our fathers,
  Protected, exalted, and blest,
O nation, where Freedom has planted
  The banner of peace and of rest,
Give thanks for a plentiful harvest,
  His name and His mercy revere,
Who prospers the hand of the toiler,
  And crowns with his goodness the year

ODE TO THANKSGIVING.

Air, "America."

Anthems to God above,
Source of eternal love,
  Now let us sing!
Praise our Creator's name,
Come as our Fathers came:
Hail and with loud acclaim
  Our Lord and King!

Thanks for our favored land,
By His Almighty hand
  Guarded from ill!

Thanks for the **dew** and rain,
Broad field and sunny plain
Where stores of fruit and grain
    Our garners fill!

Thanks for our banner bright,
Spangled with starry light,
    Boast of the free—
Signal to those oppressed,
Honored, revered, and blest,
Waving its noble crest
    O'er land and sea!

Lord, from thy throne on high
Bend thy approving eye
    O'er us, we pray!
This be our one desire:
Faith, love, and zeal inspire;
Light with devotion's fire
    Our souls today!

———

CHRISTMAS CAROL.

Air, "Portuguese Hymn."

Fulfilled is the promise, a Saviour is born:
With loud acclamation we hallow the morn!
To God in the highest all glory we sing,
And welcome the advent of Jesus, our King!

We come like the shepherds who knelt at His
        feet;

We come like the wise men our monarch to
    greet.
Our faith-star unclouded shines bright on our
    way,
And leads to the manger where cradled He lay.

Good-will from our Father and peace unto
    men :
Oh, wonderful chorus! we hear it again,
In grandeur and beauty still rolling along;
While valley and mountain break forth into
    song!

O blesséd Redeemer, by prophets foretold!
We herald the story that never grows old.
Our heart's adoration before Him we bring,
And joyful hosannas to Jesus, our King!

We come with the faithful who gather today
In grateful devotion our tribute to pay;
We come with the children our carols to sing,
And shout hallelujah to Jesus, our King!

EVENING TIME.

Melody, "Sweet Hour of Prayer."

At evening time, sweet evening time,
When memory-bells in tuneful chime
Awake the joys to which we clung,
When days were bright and life was young,
'Tis then the voice of one we love,

Whose spirit dwells in realms above,
In thought repeats from yonder clime
The prayers she taught at evening time.

'Tis wafted on the fragrant breeze,
That simple prayer whose words were these:
"And now I lay me down to sleep,
I pray the Lord my soul to keep."
A mother's form, a mother's face,
Her tender look and gentle grace,
With memory-bells that softly chime,
Come back to us at evening time.

They come like balm and lull to rest
The aching brow and throbbing breast;
We feel her arms around us thrown,
And how her love is still our own.
Ah, soon we'll gladly clasp her hand
Amid the flowers of Eden land,
Where memory-bells forever chime
Beyond the shades of evening time!

FROM STAR TO STAR.

Melody, "Autumn."

There are voices—happy voices—
    And our hearts with joy they fill,
When our faith is looking upward,
    And the busy world is still:
How we listen to their music
    From our Father's home afar,

Where on Love's eternal mission,
　　We shall roam from star to star!

There are voices—gentle voices—
　　And we hear them in a dream,
Like the carol of a birdling
　　Or the murmur of a stream:
And they draw our spirits nearer
　　To the pearly gates afar,
Where among the just made perfect,
　　We shall roam from star to star!

There are voices—kindred voices—
　　And they call from yonder shore
Where our golden harps will waken
　　Songs we never knew before:
Oh, the rapture that awaits us
　　In the glory-land afar
Where together and forever
　　We shall roam from star to star!

————

TRUSTING.

Air, "Day and Night thy Lambs Are Crying."

I am trusting, O my Saviour!
　　I am trusting only thee;
I have proved thy gracious promise—
　　As my day my strength shall be.
I am trusting, O my Saviour!
　　Though my path I may not know;
When thou callest, I will answer;
　　Where thou leadest, I will go.

147

I am trusting, O my Saviour!
  And my hand is firm in thine;
Though the clouds may sometimes gather,
  Still I see thy glory shine.
And I look beyond the shadows
  To the sunny fields of rest,
And I catch the glad hosannas
  Of the faithful and the blest.

I am trusting, O my Saviour!
  I am trusting day by day;
Holy angels guard my footsteps,
  And I cannot lose my way.
For thy spirit hovers o'er me,
  Like a pure and gentle dove; .
And in all my cares and sorrows,
  I can hear His voice of love.

Like the early dews of morning,
  How thy precious gifts descend!
And I know that thou art with me
  And will keep me to the end.
In thy secret place abiding,
  Oh the joy thy presence brings!
I am covered with thy feathers—
  I am safe beneath thy wings!

TO THE RESCUE.

Air, "All the Way My Saviour Leads Me."

Oh, the sad and troubled faces
  That we meet from day to day,
And the hearts that break in silence

As they plod their dreary way!
Can we pass them by unheeded;
　　Can we leave them still alone,
When 'tis ours to scatter roses
　　Where relentless thorns are strown?

With an earnest prayerful spirit,
　　In the name of Christ our Lord,
Let us ask if we are living
　　As He taught us in His word.
Have we fed the poor and clothed them
　　As the Saviour gave command?
To reclaim an erring brother
　　Have we lent a helping hand?

Oh, the homes that we may comfort,
　　Homes where want and sorrow dwell!
If unfaithful to the Master,
　　Can we say with us 'tis well?
To the rescue let us hasten,
　　Ere the warning sun goes down:
Lest our work be left unfinished,
　　And another take our crown!

———

GOD'S LIGHT OF PROMISE.

Air, "Webb."

Rejoice, rejoice, O pilgrim!
　　Lift up thine eyes and see
Above the mist and shadows
　　A light that shines for thee!
'Tis God's own light of Promise—
　　His smile of perfect peace:

And soon with Him forever
　　Thy weary march will cease.

Rejoice, rejoice, O pilgrim,
　　And hail the blessed light,
Whose radiant beams are leading
　　Beyond the veil of night!
Let love thy soul inspiring
　　Thy faith and hope increase
Till safe among the ransomed
　　Thy weary march shall cease!

Rejoice, rejoice, O pilgrim:
　　The Master's work fulfil!
The light that cheers thy pathway
　　Is growing brighter still!
Press onward, O press onward
　　To realms of perfect peace,
When in thy Father's kingdom
　　Thy weary march shall cease!

———

THERE ARE MOMENTS.

Tune, "Shall We Know Each Other There?"

There are moments—blesséd moments—
　　That in spirit we recall;
There are seasons of refreshing—
　　Oh how precious to us all!
When we feel the sacred presence
　　Of our great High Priest and King,
And as if by inspiration
　　Of His wondrous love we sing!

There are moments—blessèd moments—
  When a radiance from the skies
Seems to burst in all its glory
  On our faith-illumined eyes;
And we hear a voice proclaiming,
  While in song our voices blend,
"I am Alpha and Omega,
  The beginning and the end."

There are moments—blessèd moments—
  When such perfect joy we see,
That we stand upon the threshold
  Of a life that soon shall be;
And again the Master speaketh
  While in silent prayer we blend:
He again confirms the promise,
  "I am with you to the end!"

CHAPTER XXVII.—1903.

A POEM BY MARGARET E. SANGSTER.

WHILE this book was in preparation, its publishers wrote, without my previous knowledge, to my dear friend Mrs. Sangster, for a poem to appear in its pages. I understand that within a few hours the gifted poet had written and mailed the following lines, which, as in the previous cases in this book, I include with no other feeling than thankfulness for the kind and partial friends that God has raised up around me:

The dear Lord has kept her close to Him,
  In a little curtained space
That never is wholly dusk or dim,
  Because of His shining face;
Though we are afraid of the brooding dark
  It cannot be so to her,
For the Lord Himself has made an ark
  For His loving worshipper.

There are things of earth that she cannot see,
  Except with her spirit's eyes;
The light in the blossom-perfumed tree,
  The stars in the still night-skies;

152

Poem by Margaret E. Sangster.

But never imagine she has not known
  Far fairer sights than ours!
The hem of His garment round her thrown
  Is broidered with fadeless flowers.

She smiles the smile of a happy child,
  Her voice as the child's is sweet,
She has followed so safe through wood and
     wild,
  The print of her Saviour's feet.
Her ear, attuned to the finest chord,
  Has caught the songs of heaven;
She has taught us all how to praise her Lord
  For the grace of sins forgiven.

Her song has bubbled with notes of joy,
  Has risen in faith so strong,
It has reached the height where the whole em-
     ploy
  Is praise, where the ransomed throng.
And year by year as the sifted snow
  Of age on her head is white,
She has been as a child of the long ago,
  In her dear Lord's loving sight.

Why call her blind, who can see so well
  The hidden things and clear:
Who knows so much that she may not tell,
  Of the land that's drawing near?
The pure in heart, our Saviour said,
  And the word is true for aye,
Though drifting centuries on have sped,
  Since He went to His home on high,

The pure in heart shall *see*, ah! yes,
  They shall see the face of Him
Who dwells forever in ceaseless bliss
  Between the cherubim.
Of her we love, this wondrous word
  Is true in very deed.
'Tis the sight of her own, her loving Lord,
  In her sightless eyes we read.

God bless her ever! we lift the prayer—
  Our hearts would hold her, fain
To guard her now from the weight of care,
  To shield her life from pain.
And when at last an angel comes
  To lead her in to the King,
God give her a place in the best of homes
  Where the choiring angels sing!

May the thin veil drop from the gentle eyes,
  And by the King's own grace
When she sees Him, clear, with no surprise,
  May she have a sheltered place
In a little corner white and fair,
  And very near His feet:
And never a voice 'mid the voices there,
  Shall ring more true and sweet!

CHAPTER XXVIII.—1903.

L IVING and learning still, in this year of
our Lord, 1903, I have again and
again to repeat the words that were
flashed over the wires in the very
first telegram ever sent: "What hath God
wrought!"

At the time I made my little excursion down
the Hudson River (narrated in a preceding
chapter), in search of physical light, there was
not a single locomotive in this country, and
no immediate prospect that there would ever
be any. There was just one little railroad,
four miles long: and that ran from Quincy,
Mass., to the ocean, and its cars were used for
the purpose of transporting granite from the
quarries to a landing, where it could be placed

upon ships, which should carry it to different parts of the world.

It was not until 1827, when I was seven years old, that news went through the country, of two men having been sent to England, to buy some locomotives! They were not very "flush" with them, over there: but these messengers from the Western Republic succeeded in getting three of the desired articles, for use on the Delaware and Hudson Railroad.

And what queer little creatures they were, as we remember the descriptions of them, and compare them with what now exists!—although they probably looked very large and imposing, to people who had never seen anything greater than wagons and carriages. No doubt many of the automobiles of today are larger and stronger than were those locomotives, which had only four wheels apiece, and were small in proportion.

But these were, so to speak, the progenitors of others: a flock of them soon appeared. In 1830, when I was ten years old, news came that Peter Cooper, afterwards famous for the founding of the Cooper Institute, in New York City, had really built an engine of his own, at Baltimore, instead of sending to England for it.

He soon took the famous trip from Albany to Schenectady and back, on what is now a part of the great New York Central and Hudson River system: and a great contrast that little outfit (so well known by pictures of it) would be, to the swift and heavy express-

trains that now rush along those tracks!
"What hath God wrought!"

There are now, probably, over a hundred
thousand miles of railway in this country, and
considerably more than twenty thousand locomotives. It is something to have lived long
enough to witness all this change and growth!

When I first went to school, in New York,
and for many years afterward, there was no
way of communicating with my friends at
home, excepting by the mail-coach or by private messenger: and that took a long and tedi-
ous time, compared to present methods and
facilities. Often, when friends and relatives
lived at some distance from each other, one
would be dead and buried before the other
even knew that anything was amiss.

As railroads multiplied, the means for dis-
seminating news became better and better:
but it was not until 1844, that the first tele-
graphic message was sent.

What changes have taken place since, in
that respect! Now we can send long commu-
nications in a few seconds, almost anywhere
in the civilized world; now we can even throw
our voices, through the wonderful ventrilo-
quism of the telephone, hundreds and eve·
thousands of miles; now people upon ships
are communicating with each other and with
people on the shore, by means of wireless telegraphy, all the way across the ocean.

Not only can intelligence be communicated
to and fro with astonishing quickness, but the
great events of the preceding day are spread

before the people, as soon as they are up in
the morning. Everybody that can read, has
this luxury—from the millionaire in his man-
sion, to the workman going to his early morning task. "What hath God wrought!"

Thousands of other improvements I might
mention—the absence and the beginnings of
which, I can well recollect. The drawing-
room car, the sleeping-car, the air-brake (by
which many lives have been saved), the phono-
graph, the moving picture, the bicycle, the
typewriter, the X-ray, the elevator, the sew-
ing-machine, the parlor- and safety-match,
anæsthetics, the reaper and mower, the sub-
marine boat, the type-setting machine (with
which this very book is "set up")—all these,
and many others, have been invented within
the span of my lifetime.

During the past ten years, and up to the
present time, my life has continued to be, for
the most part, one of joy and sunshine. I do
not write quite so much as in other days, but
have not by any means laid my pen aside
From the vantage-ground of eighty-three
years, I look back upon fair and peaceful val-
leys, plains, and hillsides, covered by flowers.
interspersed with only now and then a thorn.

My health continues, as has been almost
constantly the case for many years, good and
sound; my spirits are every bit as light and
gay as during my girlhood; my enjoyment of
all the blessings of life, is more full and intense
than ever.

Among my audiences at various places,

158

during lecture-trips, I am continually meeting old acquaintances, who recall former scenes, and enable me to live them over again. I also meet many new friends, who profess themselves to have been for many years drawn toward me by my hymns.

Many words of love and appreciation are constantly falling upon my ears; and I feel that it is truly the Lord's hand that leads me.

It has been my privilege to visit the Northfield Convention, that famous institution founded by the late D. L. Moody, for several years in succession; I often attend other summer conventions of the kind. In these, I am enabled to address large audiences, who always listen to my humble words with close and respectful attention.

It is an addition to the pleasure of these occasions, that I am thus enabled to hear some of the best orators and musicians that the world affords; and keep pace, as well as my poor abilities are able, with the thought and feeling of the centuries.

I had for many years lived in Brooklyn, which I found a very pleasant locality, and where I have many dear and treasured friends, whom I still visit from time to time; but three years ago it was considered best for my health that I remove to Bridgeport, Conn., and make my home with a widowed sister, who has been a lifelong resident of that city. I find that the change has been decidedly beneficial.

A great deal has often been said about "the infirmities of age", and "the decline of life";

but I believe that we are really "as young as we feel", and that while I continue to do good for the sake of it and for the love of it, the sunshine of hope and gladness will ever attend my footsteps.

I believe myself still really in the prime of life: ready to take up any duty that suggests itself, and to do it with my utmost strength. I do not at this age feel any more fatigue from my frequent journeys and efforts before audiences, than I did thirty years ago. My work grows sweeter and grander to me each day; and I believe the public, in buying large numbers of this my Life-Story, will show that it means to encourage and sustain me in it.

I am often asked, "How long do you expect to live?" This question, of course, I cannot accurately answer: but am willing to stay as long as the good Lord has any work for me to do; and have "set the mark" at one hundred and three—the age at which my grandmother died—my mother living to be over ninety. My ancestors were Puritans; my family tree is rooted around Plymouth Rock; all my predecessors of lineage died at a good old age. Whenever the Lord calls me, I am willing to go; but if He chooses to leave me here until the above-mentioned time, or even longer, I shall continue to gather sheaves till the sun goes down, and to sing and write hymns to His praise.

THE END.

Made in the USA
Las Vegas, NV
22 August 2022

53729441R00096